BEYOND HOPE

BEYOND HOPE

An Illustrated History of the Fraser and Cariboo Gold Rush

Beverley Boissery *and* **Bronwyn Short**

THE DUNDURN GROUP
TORONTO

Copy-Editor: Jennifer Bergeron
Design: Jennifer Scott
Printer: University of Toronto Press

National Library of Canada Cataloguing in Publication Data

Boissery, Beverley, 1939-
  Beyond hope: an illustrated history of the Fraser and Cariboo Gold Rush/ Beverley Boissery and Bronwyn Short.

Includes bibliographical references.
ISBN 1-55002-471-X

1. Fraser River Valley (B.C.) — Gold discoveries — Pictorial works. 2. Cariboo (B.C. : Regional district) — Gold discoveries — Pictorial works. I. Short, Bronwyn II. Title.

FC3820.G6B63 2003   971.1'37   C2003-904045-3

1   2   3   4   5   07   06   05   04   03

 Canadä

We acknowledge the support of the **Canada Council for the Arts** and the **Ontario Arts Council** for our publishing program. We also acknowledge the financial support of the **Government of Canada** through the **Book Publishing Industry Development Program** and **The Association for the Export of Canadian Books**, and the **Government of Ontario** through the **Ontario Book Publishers Tax Credit** program, and the **Ontario Media Development Corporation's Ontario Book Initiative.**

Care has been taken to trace the ownership of copyright material used in this book. The author and the publisher welcome any information enabling them to rectify any references or credit in subsequent editions.

J. Kirk Howard, President

Printed and bound in Canada.✪
Printed on recycled paper.
www.dundurn.com

Dundurn Press
8 Market Street
Suite 200
Toronto, Ontario, Canada
M5E 1M6

Dundurn Press
2250 Military Road
Tonawanda NY
U.S.A. 14150

For Dave
the best of friends

PREFACE

For the purposes of consistency, we have used Vancouver Island (rather than its earlier form Vancouver's Island) and Esquimalt (which was sometimes spelled Esquimault) throughout.

In the 1850s, £1 was the equivalent of $5. Monetary sums throughout the book are given in the values of the gold rush era when, generally speaking, one ounce of gold sold for US$17.50. This is a far cry from today's price of more than US$350.

ACKNOWLEDGEMENTS

Although we have been greatly helped by a number of librarians and archivists, we can acknowledge the professional assistance of only a few: Patricia Kennedy and Andrew Rodger of the National Archives of Canada; Shiri Alon of the McCord Museum; Lyn Moranda of the Vancouver Museum Archives; Julie Warren and Kelly-Ann Nolin of the Royal British Columbia Museum for help on the photographs; the Mitchell Library, Sydney, New South Wales and the State Archives of New South Wales; and Catherine Whiteley of the Malaspina University College library.

We are also grateful to the following institutions for permission to publish various images: the State Library of Victoria; the Bancroft Library, University of California, Berkeley; and Hancock House. We thank Alden and Cali Hackman for permission to use Tim Crosby's photograph of the hurdy-gurdy and Heritage House for the use of maps from Branwen Patenaude's *Trails to Gold*, published by Horsdal and Schubart.

As well, we would like to thank Kirk Howard and Tony Hawke for their encouragement and Jennifer Bergeron for her editorial expertise. Writing for Dundurn was a pleasure.

Our gratitude to Chris Greenwood for diligent proofreading. And last, but certainly not least, we thank Ben and Josh Short for their patient direction, enthusiastic support, and, most importantly, their crash course into the mysteries of cyberspace.

BEYOND HOPE

In the mid-nineteenth century one single word had the power to pull men from homes and families: *gold*. After John Marshall found nuggets in a Californian stream in 1848, tens of thousands crossed continents and oceans in the scramble for wealth. A few years later Edward Hargraves's discovery of gold near Bathurst prompted a similar rush to the Australian colonies of New South Wales and Victoria.

Stories of lawlessness in the Californian and Australian goldfields became legion. Men shot each other after hearing rumours of a new find and murdered many miners as they tried to convey their gold to safety. Shantytowns sprang up throughout the goldfields and far too many miners lost their earnings through gambling, prostitution, and drinking. Both gold rushes saw extraordinary movements of peoples and produced breathtaking stories of incredible fortunes made overnight.

A London *Punch* cartoon satirizing the Australian goldfields.

A GOLD FIELD IN THE "DIGGINS."

However, by the mid-1850s these goldfields had begun to run dry. Miners abandoned the shantytowns and new prospectors stopped arriving. Merchants who had envisaged making their fortunes through provisioning them went bankrupt, and scores of rotting ships littered the San Francisco Harbor. Thousands with nothing to offer but their experience in the mining of gold drifted from place to place, some in despair, but almost all hungry for the hint of a new chase, as the rush for gold was called.

Deserted ships in San Francisco Harbor, late 1850s.

It can be no wonder, then, that when the first stories of gold surfaced in today's British Columbia, the government took great care to keep them secret. As early as August 1850 the governor of Vancouver Island, Richard Blanshard, reported to the colonial secretary in London that he had seen "a very rich specimen of gold ore" from the Queen Charlotte Islands, and the Hudson's Bay Company sent expeditions to investigate. The company provided supplies such as explosives and mining tools for one in 1851, and forty men agreed to work for just their share of the profits. The leader of this expedition claimed British possession of the islands and drove away a party of Americans who had heard rumours of another potential goldfield.

First Nations people from the Queen Charlotte Islands. The Haida regularly traded with the Hudson's Bay Company.

Queen Charlotte gold differed from that discovered by Marshall and Hargraves. Miners called it a "blowout" because it had to be chipped or blasted from rich veins in rocks. When the Hudson's Bay men chose the latter method, they found the Haida people averse to seeing their gold being taken away so summarily. The HBC *Una's* logbook records that the Haida concealed themselves in bushes "until the report was heard and then made a rush for the gold. A regular scramble between them and our men would take place: the Indians would take our men by their legs and hold them away from the gold." This particular 1851 venture took a tremendous loss, costing the company £950 and gaining a mere £90 worth of gold. With such a return, the Hudson's Bay Company soon abandoned Queen Charlotte mining.

Dr. John Sebastian Helmcken, a Hudson's Bay Company physician and adviser of Governor James Douglas.

But other reports of gold trickled in from the mainland. Native people gave gold dust to the chief trader of Fort Kamloops, Donald McLean, in 1852, and four years later he reported that he had accumulated two bottles half full of Thompson River gold. Samples reached Victoria and in about 1857, "Governor [James] Douglas at the mess table shewed us a few grains of scale gold … This was the first gold I saw and probably the first that arrived here." According to the writer, Dr. John Helmcken: "The Governor attached great importance to it and thought that it meant change and a busy time … [with] Victoria rising to a great city." However, most residents reacted with skepticism and less excitement, thinking the governor was promoting "a sort of advertisement for 'town lots'."

They would be shaken from such complacency very rapidly after the Hudson's Bay Company sent eight hundred ounces of gold to San Francisco for assaying a year later and whispers of northern gold turned into the shout of "Gold on the Frazer." Miners dreamed again of fortunes. Men everywhere clamoured for information about this new goldfield. This confluence of events produced the flood of people that deluged Fort Victoria in the spring of 1858.

Alfred Waddington, a San Francisco merchant who hurried to establish a branch of his wholesale grocery firm in Victoria, commented that the "proximity of Victoria to San Francisco

An artist's rendering of Victoria, c. 1860.

Alfred Waddington.

... afforded every facility, and converted the matter into a fifteen dollar trip. Steamers and sailing vessels were put in requisition, and old ships and tubs of every description [became] actively employed in bringing up passengers."

Another commentator, R.M. Ballantyne, drew a vivid picture of these ships and their passengers. "A steamer calculated to carry 600 passengers," he wrote, "is laden with 1,600. There is hardly standing room on the deck. It is almost impossible to clear passage from one part of the vessel to the other. ... Their object is of the earth, earthly-wealth in its rawest and rudest form — gold, the one thing for which they bear to live, or dare to die." In their haste to reach the fabulous wealth of the Fraser and Thompson rivers, prospectors stripped stores of provisions. Whether anyone liked it or not, the secret was out and another gold rush on.

In some people's eyes, the forty-niners of California had achieved bogeyman status. Their exploits and behaviour were legendary, and people of many countries looked upon them as brutal, lawless, vicious, and wild. Armed with guns and bowie knives, they were a law unto themselves, the antithesis to the "peace, order and good government" policy of the British colonial system.

Alfred Waddington's initial impression of Victoria was that it was "a quiet village of about 800 inhabitants. No noise, no bustle, no gamblers, no speculators or interested parties to preach up this or underrate that." The well-behaved residents lived in seclusion, "as it were, from the whole world." Their reaction to the invasion of gold-obsessed Californians was therefore predictable. Emerging from church on April 25, 1858, Dr. Helmcken wrote, they "were astonished to find a steamer enter-ing the harbour from San Francisco." The *Commodore* disembarked 450 men, all heavily equipped for mining and carrying knives and guns. Waddington observed that the churchgoers "beheld these varied specimens of humanity streaming down in motley crowds from the steamers and sailing vessels … in silent amazement, as if contemplating a second eruption of the barbarians!"

On April 25, 1858, the *Commodore* disembarked 450 eager, fevered pursuers of gold, much to the astonished dismay of Victoria's residents.

While some Californian prospectors came overland from the south, Victoria bore the brunt of the influx of gold seekers. In fact, so many made their way north that the San Francisco press lamented the lost labourers and the subsequent damage to the Californian economy: "The desire to emigrate is fast increasing. … Several hundreds have left in the past fortnight and many more are preparing to leave."

To this point, the two British colonies on the northern Pacific coast — Vancouver Island and New Caledonia — were largely unknown to the wider world. Only very recently had the British navy transferred the site of its Pacific operations from Valparaiso in the southern Pacific to Esquimalt, and that was only because it needed a base closer to the Russian port of Vladivostok once the Crimean War broke out. The area was chiefly the domain of the various First Nations, although the Hudson's Bay Company had built a chain of trading posts across the north that connected to southern forts in Kamloops, Langley, and Hope.

And, of course, Fort Victoria. Established in 1842, after the loss of territory in the Oregon Treaty, it was a rough settlement with a bastion on its southwest corner and a series of wooden struc-

Hospital Point, Esquimalt Harbour, Vancouver Island, was "picturesquely rock-bound." Early arrivals found it "crowded with gracefully peaked canoes and boats of all shapes and sizes": Kinahan Cornwallis.

The Bastion, Government Street, Victoria, 1858.

tures. Its inhabitants were all connected to the HBC and the eight hundred people living there were the usual mix — Scottish officers, Canadiens, Métis, and a few Kanakas (Hawaiians).

The newcomers built a tent city around the fort and shopped for provisions. Prices for everyday basics, such as flour, soared, and the influx of miners transformed Victoria into a busy commercial centre, as described by Waddington: "Shops, stores and wooden shanties of every description were now seen going up and nothing was to be heard but the stroke of the chisel or hammer. In six weeks, 225 buildings, of which nearly 200 were stores ... had been added to the village of 800 inhabitants."

Few miners, however, allowed themselves the luxury of observing such effects. They were desperate to reach the goldfields, and the next stage of their trip required some means of transport across the Strait of Georgia to the Fraser River. They left in whatever watercraft they could find — steamers, sailboats, or canoes — and if they couldn't find anything, they built their own "punty, awkward-looking things, about as good imitations of coffins as anything else." Consequently, many perished. Today, the journey takes one hundred minutes by public ferry. In 1858, it was a two-

Bustling Victoria Harbour, August 1858 — "a trading post of the Hudson's Bay Company, bids fair, on account of its position with regard to the gold fields ... speedily to become a large town": *Illustrated London News.*

day trip, requiring an overnight stop on one of the Gulf Islands, such as Miner's Bay on Mayne Island.

But once the prospectors reached the mainland they discovered their difficulties had only just begun. The Fraser quickly narrowed into a swiftly flowing river and exacted its own death toll. As Governor Douglas reported to London: "with every species of small craft ... continually employed in pouring their cargoes of human beings into the Fraser river ... many accidents have happened in the dangerous rapids of that river." In fact, "a great number of canoes" had been "dashed to pieces and their cargoes swept away by the impetuous stream, while ... the ill-fated adventurers who accompanied them ... have been swept into eternity."

Such incidents did nothing to tarnish the lure of gold. In May 1858, 1,262 would-be miners left San Francisco. The total rose to 7,149 in June and to 6,278 in July. By the end of the year, approximately twenty-five thousand prospectors had come via that route to Victoria, and the journey to

San Francisco. W. Champness, an Englishman on his way to the Cariboo goldfields, observed that it had grown from a village in 1848 to have a population of more than 100,000 in fourteen years, concluding it "is evident that Californians live in a land where gold is prevalent." This illustration, like others that follow, was published with his story in *The Leisure Hour.*

The SS *Enterprise.*

the Fraser had been made safer with the introduction of stern-wheeled steamers, such as the *Enterprise,* captained by Tom Wright, generally acknowledged as a "prince of good fellows."

Reporter David Higgins, whose observations of the goldfields can be found in *The Mystic Spring and Other Tales of Western Life*, published in 1904.

In July 1858 a journalist, David Higgins, an eyewitness to the many exciting and tragic events of the period, described his trip to Yale, "then the head of navigation." The vessel, he wrote, "was crowded with freight and passengers and I was lucky in finding a vacant spot on the hurricane deck upon which to spread my blankets and lie down to unpleasant dreams." It took a day to reach "Fort Langley, a Hudson Bay Post, where we remained over night. New Westminster had then no existence, a dense forest of fir and cedar occupying the site of the future Royal City."

Fort Langley's gates opened each morning at six o'clock when "the massive bolts and bars are unlocked … and the English, Scotch, Irish, half-breeds, begin to make their appearance in and around the establishment. At a later hour … the door of the sales-room opens … and the business of the day begins": *Harper's Weekly*, 1858.

Just below Langley, "some speculative spirits were booming a town which they named Derby, but it was only a name" and did not last. After sailing on from Langley, "the wild scenery of course charmed all, and incidents of travel were novel and exciting to those who had not been accustomed to life outside a large city. All along the river, wherever there occurred a bench or bar, miners were encamped waiting … to scoop up the gold by the handful and live at ease forevermore."

Those miners may have been part of a group that had come overland. T.H. Hill, after noticing colours in the Fraser's water, had washed a pan of gravel and thus discovered one of the richest river bars in North America. Hill's Bar would produce more than $2 million in gold (or about US$35 million today). Seeing Hill's success, other miners staked claims up and down the lower Fraser, scattered around the settlements of Hope and Yale, which turned into bustling communities. David Higgins vividly described them: "All was a bustle and excitement in the new mining town. Every race and colour and both sexes were represented in the population. There were Englishmen, Canadians [i.e. from Upper and Lower Canada], Americans, Australians, Frenchmen, Spaniards, Mexicans, Chinese and Negroes — all bent on winning gold from the Fraser sands and all hopeful of a successful season. It was a lottery in which there were few prizes."

But a lottery, nevertheless, that all the miners thought they had a chance of winning. The lower Fraser's gold could be mined through "surface" digging. The cheapest method used involved a pan about eighteen inches wide and three or four inches deep with broad sloping sides. Miners stirred and swirled sand and gravel in the pan to separate any gold, which, because it was six times heavier than

rock, sank to the bottom. Experienced and fortunate prospectors extracted gold fairly efficiently by this method and many "panned" a site to assess its potential before staking claims. Most miners,

Hope. Bishop George Hills believed that no spot could be "more beautifully situated than Hope. The River Fraser flows past it. The site is on the river bank, on either side are noble mountains opposite an island." A less spiritual observer, writing for *Harper's Weekly*, wrote that "temporary frame buildings are going up in all directions. Gambling houses — of which there are five here — are in full blast, day and night; and the number of houses where liquor is sold is about nine out of every ten."

Fort Yale. Lieutenant Richard Mayne of the Royal Navy thought "there is nothing calling for any notice in Yale." Residents, however, disagreed. David Higgins feared "to go out after dark. Night assaults and robberies, varied by an occasional cold-blooded murder or a daylight theft, were common occurrences. Crime in every form stalked boldly through the town unchecked and unpunished."

A lithograph showing the various techniques used in Californian gold mining (clockwise, from top right): conduits, or flumes, bringing water through which gravel is sifted; miners shovelling dirt into a sluice; a windlass bringing underground dirt to the surface; a miner panning in the stream; and, on the left, a seated prospector uses a rocker.

Left: Gold mining technology spread from continent to continent. This illustration shows the gold pan as used by an Australian miner.

Right: His counterpart in British Columbia as portrayed by Overlander William Hind. W. Champness noted that a "prospecting-pan forms a first-rate dish for beans and bacon" and "is one of the most useful articles one can bring here."

however, used the faster rocker or "cradle" if they had the means and skill. Working in twos, one poured water onto the gravel while the other rocked the cradle back and forth. If they were in luck, a series of riffles caught any gold in the bottom of the box while a blanket underneath collected even the finest particles.

By June 1858 the roll of the dice seemed heavily weighted against the miners. Constantly challenged by such hazards as hypothermia and exhaustion, they now witnessed an insurmountable obstacle. Once the spring melt began, many

Left: The rocker as shown in the Australian goldfields was a more efficient method of placer gold extraction.

Right: Again, techniques crossed oceans as shown by Bill Phinney, a British Columbian equivalent of the Australian digger.

bars disappeared beneath the water and hundreds of disillusioned miners gave up their dreams and returned home to California in disgust. Others who had the patience and resources to wait out the season returned in late summer to continue mining, and several began pushing even further up the Fraser in search of a richer motherlode. As they did, the dangers multiplied.

Beyond Yale, the canyons of the river were heartbreakingly precarious, the rapids extremely dangerous, and the cliffs steep. Around the precipices wound ancient native paths.

Left: Mountain roads. "In the river gorges, our track conducted us along the most frightful precipices … down whose steep, pine-forested sides we had to lead our horses singly, and [then] with the utmost care": W. Champness.

Right: The aptly named Hell's Gate or Great Canyon confronted miners heading up the river in search of rich motherlodes. Bishop Hills, searching for a different treasure, wrote that their progress "seemed like the crawling of a fly on the perpendicular wall" frequently "hanging between life and death."

Alexander Caulfield Anderson, explorer, surveyor, and chief factor of HBC Fort Colville, authored a *Handbook and Map to the Gold Region* — one of many guides written to aid miners in their quest for gold.

Sometimes, even such narrow trails were nonexistent. Many miners and their horses, cruelly loaded with huge, three-hundred-pound packs, perished in the jaws of the river while attempting to claw their way around these paths. The further up the canyon they progressed, the harder the maintenance of vital supplies became. But despite such perils to life and limb, many succeeded in their trek to the upper Fraser. Their stories lured others — those obsessed with dreams of richer strikes.

As the volume of prospectors and the subsequent toll of lives multiplied, Governor Douglas realized something urgently needed to be done. He decided to bypass the Fraser Canyon and build a road over a track first explored by Alexander Caulfield Anderson of the HBC in 1846. Under Anderson's supervision, five hundred miners during

Map showing the preferred route to the upper Fraser before the building of the Cariboo trail.

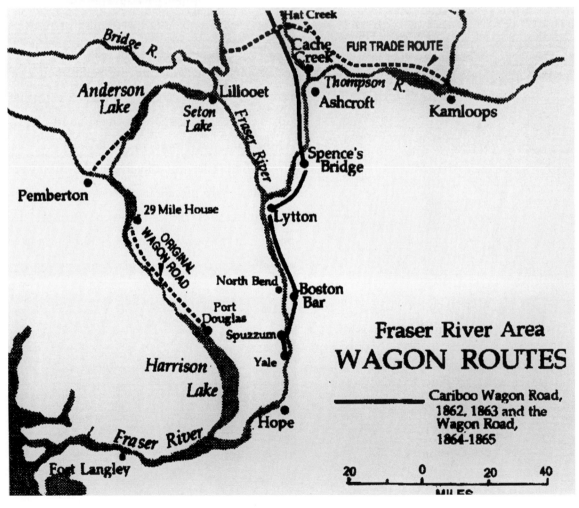

Fraser River Area
WAGON ROUTES

—————— Cariboo Wagon Road, 1862, 1863 and the Wagon Road, 1864-1865

a five-month period in 1858 carved a mule trail four feet wide along the portages of the Harrison-Lillooet route.

Astoundingly, labourers from every corner of the globe volunteered to help perform this amazing feat, and in return the government paid for their transportation (which took them part-way to the goldfields), equipment, and food. Many praised this first road into the interior of British Columbia as a historical and prodigious achievement, although some experienced HBC men scoffed at its engineering. The road's construction, imperfect as it was, radically reduced the cost of the trip to the upper Fraser both in dollars and, more importantly, lives.

Lytton. The small settlement of Lytton had little to commend itself to visitors. Lieutenant Mayne described it as consisting of "an irregular row of some dozen wooden huts, a drinking saloon, an express office, a large court-house — as yet unfinished — and two little buildings near the river." Mayne and his companions were "pleased to leave the dust and wind of Lytton." Bishop Hills, uncharacteristically, seemed to have forgotten to pack his rose-coloured glasses: "We left Lytton without regret. It is a cold, windy, unsheltered flat and the people more alien than any place I have ever been."

By the end of 1859, the centre of mining had shifted from Hope and Yale to the areas around Lytton and Lillooet. Other places, such as Port Douglas on the shores of Harrison Lake, became busy centres of activity as they provisioned the almost constant stream of men on their way to the goldfields. As most prospectors abandoned the lower Fraser's bars, Chinese miners, who had abandoned California where hostile legislation made their lives difficult, moved in. With a patience not shown by other miners, they toiled for smaller returns until the diggings ran dry.

Unlike Lytton, Lillooet received high praise from Mayne: "Lillooet is a very pretty site, on the whole decidedly the best I saw on the Fraser River." It has "now grown into a somewhat important town, situated as it is, at the north end of the Harrison-Lillooet route, at its junction with the Fraser."

Left: Fort Douglas, established after the building of the Douglas road, was not a favoured stop for travellers. George Blair described it as "a nasty, dirty little place with ten or twelve houses or hovels, chiefly gambling-holes." Bishop Hills, as usual, had a different view to most. Overwhelmed by the magnificence of Harrison Lake, he wrote about "the harbour of Douglas with the town at its extremity … [which] consisted … of a few wooden buildings with an excellent quay."

Right: First Nations village. "This … village … inhabited by 200 or 300 people [who] … like all those to be met with on this route, are peaceable, intelligent, and industrious, often rendering great assistance to the traveller by carrying his baggage over land portages."

LEARNING FROM PAST MISTAKES

In the 1850s the Colonial Office, which supervised all British colonies, proved itself the rarest of all institutions when it became capable of learning. No better example can be given than the way it guided Governor James Douglas's actions in the first phases of the gold rush.

The Australian goldfields had taught Britain some bitter lessons. Douglas applied four to British Columbia. He proclaimed Crown ownership of minerals, required ownership of licences for miners, and created gold commissioners. Furthermore, an experience called the Eureka Stockade had to be avoided at all costs. In Ballarat, Victoria, previously law-abiding British subjects had united with perceived Irish and American troublemakers to riot against the gold commissioners' harsh enforcement of their regulations in 1854. Other problems contributed to the unrest as well, such as weak governance, police desertion, and demands for political change.

A close comparison of the regulations printed on mining licences from 1853 Victoria and those issued for mining in "the Couteau and Fraser's River District" of 1858 confirms London's determination not to repeat the Ballarat problems. Although much of the wording remained the same — for example, that Sunday was to be observed as a day of rest — there were significant differences. Licences were non-transferable in British Columbia and the size of claims increased dramatically. Victorian regulations

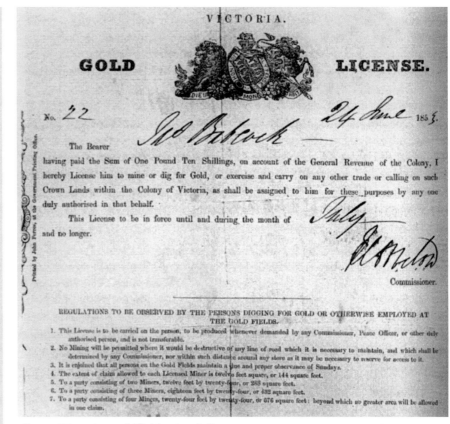

Above: Victorian goldfield miner's licence.

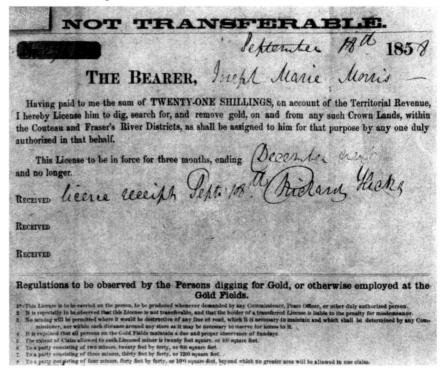

Above: British Columbia licence.

limited a group of four miners to 576 square feet. That size was more than doubled to 1,600 square feet in British Columbia.

The Gold Fields Act of 1859 was another example of building on colonial experience. Chief Justice Matthew Begbie claimed to have based it "on the model of the New Zealand mining laws: with some modifications." Governor Douglas, however, told Sir Henry Barkley, his counterpart in Victoria, that the act had "been framed on the experience of the Australian Colonies, and principally on that of Victoria." There would be no repeat of the Eureka Stockade. American miner James Bell was just one who commented on "the simplicity, promptness, and honesty with which government business was managed" in British Columbia.

Douglas and Begbie deserve high praise for the prompt establishment of law and order. Not only were the laws effective, but Begbie himself made stop after stop on his circuit through the colony to meet with miners and explain their rights and changes in the laws. By taking such steps, he ensured that lawlessness was kept to a minimum.

The huge influx of men flung the infant colony into accelerated development, and both the mainland and Vancouver Island faced unforeseen challenges. Governor James Douglas looked to the British government for help. Laws, infrastructures, and order required money, skilled management, and labour for which Douglas made desperate appeals. Help would arrive later in the year, but in the meantime Douglas used his forceful personality, experience, and knowledge of the Californian and Australian goldfields to manage the situation. He introduced a miner's licence, initially charging ten shillings a month for it, then dropping the price to one

Sir James Douglas, first governor of the colony of British Columbia, was both praised and criticized by his peers. Alfred Waddington wrote: "His acts though tardy have been judicious and liberal, considering circumstances and the many difficulties he has had to contend with. He knows the country thoroughly, was the founder and originator of Victoria, and his best interests and affections belong here. Attached as he has been and still is to the HBC, he has a hard game to play as colonial governor."

pound annually because of difficulties in collecting the money. The fee had a dual purpose. Besides providing the colony with a necessary source of income, it also reminded the miners, most of whom were American, that they were in British territory and that the gold belonged to the Crown.

Fearing a repetition of the Oregon experience, where Britain lost its claim to the land between British Columbia and the mouth of the Columbia River to American settlers, Douglas used two military vessels to control access points to the river and also to enforce the sole trading rights of the HBC on the mainland.

Douglas also had to manage the growing tensions between the First Nations peoples and the miners as they increasingly crossed paths and clashed. Previously the traders of the HBC and the Native people had enjoyed a comparatively easy-going relationship that benefited both. This changed as the volume of avaricious miners increased and their search for gold spread further and further, creating increasing conflict. On one occasion this erupted into what became known as the Boston Bar Battle, followed by a series of other incidents leading to several deaths. Only the inter-

Boston Bar in the Fraser River, twenty-five miles above Yale. Its rich gravel provoked one of the first conflicts between the miners and First Nations people. Several deaths occurred before HBC officials negotiated an uneasy peace.

Left: Colonel Richard Moody, Royal Engineers. Sent from England to assist Douglas in governing the fledgling colony, he was competent but not universally respected, although he was the chief commissioner of lands and works and lieutenant-governor of the colony. He commanded the Columbia detachment of the engineers.

Centre: Henry Spencer Palmer surveyed most of the interior of British Columbia. A man of many talents, he was instrumental in producing a handwritten weekly journal, *The Emigrant Soldiers' Gazette and Cape Horn Chronicle*, which entertained and educated his colleagues on the long trip from London to Victoria in 1858.

Right: Lieutenant Charles Wilson, whose role in enforcing the law proved invaluable, observed: "Where there is so much young blood and no female population — there are sometimes very fierce scenes enacted and the bowie knife and revolver which every man wears are in constant requisition." In the formerly law-abiding Victoria, "the whiz of revolver bullets round you goes on all day and if anyone gets shot of course it's his own fault!" A talented engineer, he contributed much to the young colony and went on to have a distinguished career, rising to the rank of major-general and receiving many awards, such as K.C.B., K.C.M.G., F.R.S., D.C.L., LL.D., and M.E.

Bottom Left: Richard Wolfenden became the Queen's Printer in charge of the Royal Engineers' printing press after first serving as Moody's gardener. He, with several others, took advantage of promised land grants and chose to settle in the colony permanently when the regiment was recalled to England in 1863.

vention of Hudson's Bay officials, whom the Natives trusted, led to an uneasy peace settlement in 1858. Again Douglas appealed to Britain for help, making the case that the goldfields presented a long-term, dangerous situation if proper management and control remained non-existent.

London listened, and help finally arrived in the form of a regiment of Royal Engineers under the command of Colonel Richard Clement Moody. The Royal Engineers were an elite corps with advancement by merit, rather than the then-usual practice of buying promotion. This regiment was, of course, a competent military force, and further,

they consisted of handpicked, multitalented volunteers with the range of skills necessary for building British Columbia into a settled colony — surveying, engineering, carpentry, printing, and church building. Sir E. Lytton, the Colonial Secretary, boasted about their "superior discipline and intelligence … which afford ground for expecting that they will be far less likely than ordinary soldiers of the line to yield to the temptation to desertion offered by the goldfields." In fact, Lytton went on, "Their capacity at once to provide for themselves in a country without habitation, appears to me to render them especially suited for this duty."

Moody would have an immediate impact on the colony, as would two other men sent by London. His first duty was to select a capital city for British Columbia, and he rejected Fort Langley for both military reasons and its proximity to the United States. Eventually he chose the site of New Westminster — a name chosen by Queen Victoria over "Queensborough" after much heated debate amongst British

Aside from their other duties, the Royal Engineers also built the first five Anglican churches in the colony. This is Holy Trinity, New Westminster. When the very positive Bishop George Hills laid its cornerstone May 22, 1860, he enthused that "the site of the new church is a very beautiful one in Victoria Gardens and commands an extensive view and will be a prominent object from the river to steamers arriving from the sea." He noted, however, "At present two deep ravines are on either side. Around are huge stumps and the grounds are entirely unlevelled."

New Westminster as viewed from the Surrey side of the Fraser in 1862. Chosen by Colonel Moody in 1858 over Fort Langley as the site for the capital of British Columbia, New Westminster became known as the "City of Stumps." The feat of clearing the mighty forest of enormous trees fell to the Royal Engineers, and Mayne wrote: "The severity of that labour, no one unacquainted with clearing bush as it exists in British Columbia can form any accurate conception."

Columbians. London sent Chartres Brew to become inspector of police. A chief justice would be among the last to arrive in 1858. Sent to establish British law order as firmly and rapidly as possible, Matthew Baillie Begbie would need all his legal skill as well as his physical stature and love of adventure to achieve this aim. During his career he often traversed the miners' routes — and they were not paths for the faint of heart!

Chartres Brew. British Columbia's first police inspector was graphically initiated into the perils and challenges faced by those seeking to reach the Fraser goldfields. En route the ship on which he travelled caught fire and capsized. Brew was one of only 68 of 560 passengers to survive. During his years of service, the chief obstacle he faced in establishing a police force was ironically the Governor himself. Douglas had not supported his appointment and, consequently, believing that the colony needed a military rather than civil police force, regularly resisted Brew's appeals for men and money.

Matthew Baillie Begbie. The first chief justice of British Columbia thrived on the challenge of establishing and enforcing British law on the goldfields of the Fraser and Cariboo regions. His responsibilities entailed making circuits over thousands of miles through the wilderness. One of his associates, Arthur Busby, wrote, "Begbie was the best of travelling companions: hardy, adaptable and better still, useful … when on circuit he lived off the country by fishing, shooting, and could steer or paddle a canoe down a swift river as well as anyone." Though not without his critics, residents and visitors alike acknowledged his part in taming the lawlessness of the goldfields. One tourist, Walter Cheadle, passing Begbie on the trail noted, "Everybody praises his just severity as the salvation of the Caribou [sic] and terror of rowdies."

Douglas put Begbie to work within days of his arrival. In a ceremony at Fort Langley, he performed his first act as chief justice, officially proclaiming the establishment of British Columbia, appointing Douglas as its first governor, and revoking the exclusive trading rights of the Hudson's Bay Company. Within weeks, the determination, resourcefulness, and abilities of Brew, Begbie, and Moody and his engineers were tested through an incident known as the "Ned McGowan War."

This so-called war involving the miners of Hill's Bar and Yale was one of the few incidents that required the military services of the Royal Engineers. It would end the era of self-rule among the mining camps on the lower Fraser, a carry-over from the Californian goldfields — as was the trouble that began at Hill's Bar. There, miners guilty of various forms of mischief and crime had come under the leadership of Ned McGowan. Although charming and persuasive, McGowan was both unscrupulous and well known to police in California. He was also well known to miners in Yale who had previously been members of Californian vigilante committees. The smouldering tension that existed between the two groups finally flared into flame when a Hill's Bar resident assaulted a Yale miner on Christmas Day, 1858.

Until Brew could assemble and train his police force, the gold commissioners had provided law and order on the goldfields as part of their mining regulation responsibilities. Hastily appointed, without much vetting, many were unsuitable — as in the case of W.P. Whannell, an Australian, who had been appointed in Yale. Whannell arrived in the colony with letters of introduction and spuriously claimed to be an officer in the Victorian Yeomanry Cavalry. He had abandoned his family when he left Australia and the woman he called his wife was, in fact, a mistress. The reporter Higgins described him as being "wont to strut about in uniform which he said he had worn in the Crimea but several … who had served in the Crimea declared it was a sergeant's uniform. … All agreed that he was no gentleman and therefore no captain." Higgins concluded: "His arrogant and oppressive conduct soon made him the most unpopular man in Yale."

At Hill's Bar, where George Perrier presided as gold commissioner, the situation was not much better, and the inept handling of the assault by these two guaranteed that the incident would rapidly get out of hand. As it did when McGowan organized a posse and rode into Yale to take the law into his own hands. Whannell hurriedly appealed to Douglas for help in a letter that verged on hysteria: "This town and district are in a state bordering on anarchy; my own and the lives of the citizens are in immediate peril." He begged for prompt aid: "An effective blow must at once be struck on the operations of these outlaws, else I tremble for the welfare of this colony."

Your friend,
Edward McGowan

Ned McGowan, lawyer, politician, and editor, was one of the most colourful and notorious figures on the Fraser goldfields. Called the "Chief of Vultures" in California, his reputation followed him to Hill's Bar, where he quickly established himself among other disreputable miners. Trouble was not slow in arriving. After the trial by Justice Begbie, which McGowan thoroughly enjoyed and during which he charmingly apologized for his misconduct, he and his associates entertained the judge and Lieutenant Mayne, who claimed, "All things considered, I have rarely lunched with a better-spoken, pleasanter party."

Yale became a gathering place for miners from all over the world, particularly the Californian Vigilante Committee. The fact that they were deeply hated by the Hill's Bar miners located just down the river meant inevitable clashes. This conflict and its violent eruption became the first incident requiring the military and judicial services of the Royal Engineers, the Chief Justice and the Police Inspector. The firm yet just handling of the affair established British law amongst the miners where previously the law of the gun had held sway.

After Whannell claimed that the Hill's Bar renegades planned to overturn British rule and annex the colony to the United States, Douglas promptly dispatched Begbie, Brew, and Moody and his engineers to take control. In wintry conditions, their journey bordered on the heroic. In an attempt to gain first-hand information before taking dramatic action, Begbie and Moody left the detachment at Fort Hope and went on together to Yale where, to their surprise, they found the town in a state of relative quiet. When McGowan struck again the next day, they

Lieutenant Richard Charles Mayne acquitted himself admirably during the disturbance known as the Ned McGowan War. While serving aboard the HMS *Plumper*, he was sent together with fifty marines to help the Royal Engineers. After Moody and his men became marooned on the *Enterprise* he, Mayne, and Chief Justice Begbie travelled to Yale by whaleboat. His presence in the colony is permanently acknowledged by the name Mayne Island, one of the Gulf Islands.

The first bishop of the new colony, George Hills, installed and sent out in 1859, served the spiritual needs of early British Columbians until 1892. His vivid diaries provide a first-hand window into the daily lives of people from all strata of society.

immediately sent for reinforcements, and the residents of Yale were thus treated to the grand sight of 125 sappers and marines in full uniform marching into town under the command of Captain John Grant. Higgins, for one, was relieved: "I never felt happier in my life than when early one morning I saw the Redcoats trekking along the opposite side of the river."

With order quickly restored, Begbie held court. The recalcitrants paid fines, McGowan made eloquent speeches, and it soon became clear that the Californians intended to submit to the governor's authority. After the trial, Ned McGowan treated his "guests" to a champagne lunch where speeches and toasts were made. Begbie received a demonstration of gold panning by the Hill's Bar miners and, in his follow-up report, recommended that Douglas appoint more competent officials to act as justices of the peace. Within a year, the calibre of men responsible for local justice radically changed, for the better.

Overblown and exaggerated though the whole incident proved to be, the handling of the so-called war proved to be a turning point in British control of the new colony. From that moment, everyone understood that the governor and his representatives had full control of law and order and that the rule of the gun would not be tolerated. Moreover, the American miners understood that they were guests in a British territory, according to an interested observer, Bishop George Hills.

Hills, sent from England to provide spiritual oversight for the far-flung colony, was one of the later arrivals and thus disembarked in Esquimalt. He then walked three miles into Victoria, "deep in mud, the like of which no one in England could imagine." However, he was not as badly off as others because "I had my long boots on … but it was hard work and thus mudded … did I make my way." The short three-mile trek would prove good practice, for Hills regularly visited all parts of his far-flung mission field, and because he spoke with everyone, regardless of wealth or social standing, his diaries provided a unique perspective. After visiting Yale on his first annual circuit to the goldfields, he summarized the new situation as being a very positive one because "all feeling of disaffection had now vanished. A change had come over [the] Americans and they were valuing more the security and genuine freedom of British rule."

Along with such improvements, rapid changes also occurred because of private initiatives. Many miners quickly realized that the only certain money to be made from the goldfields came from providing the vast array of goods and services needed by miners. With the Hudson's Bay monopoly removed, store owners, saloon and hotel managers, steamship operators, mule packers, express riders, banks, and carriage companies sprang up — such as the Barnard Express Company, operated by prominent Yale businessman, F.J. Barnard.

DIETZ & NELSON'S
British Columbia and Victoria
EXPRESS!
CONNECTING AT VICTORIA WITH

WELLS, FARGO & CO.,

For California, Oregon, Atlantic States and Europe,

AND AT YALE AND LILLOOET WITH

BARNARDS' CARIBOO EXPRESS,

For Cariboo and the Northern Mines.

CONVEYING Treasure, Valuables, Letters, Packages, and Parcels;
PURCHASING of Drafts and Bills of Exchange from Wells, Fargo & Co., and other Banking Houses;
COLLECTING Drafts, Notes of Hand, Debts, &c.;
EXECUTING Commissions, Orders, Enquiries;
FORWARDING of Merchandise, Packages, Parcels, &c.;
ATTENDING to the Registration of Mortgages, Deeds, and other Documents, the Assaying of Gold Dust, Silver, and other Ores;
PARTICULAR attention given to the purchasing of Goods at New Westminster, B.C., and Victoria, V.I., on the most favorable terms, and shipping to destination;
LANDING WARRANTS Prepared, and Goods passed through the Custom House without delay.
New Westminster, March 13, 1863.   jy24

Advertisement for express companies.

Frank J. Barnard followed the lure of gold to the Fraser, but struck it rich by establishing the Barnard Express system of transportation. Fondly known as the BX, it became famous for its efficiency and enjoyed a near monopoly on the Cariboo route.

Some chose private enterprise rather than face the rigours of a miner's life. Charles Evans, who travelled towards the goldfields via New York in 1862, may well have had the shortest mining career in B.C. history. After enduring the long sea journey, suffering bouts of seasickness and the rough conditions aboard ship, he wrote in his journal: "May 7th. Arrived at Esquimault about 1 o'clock a.m. Came ashore about 4 o'clock. Shouldered our dunnage and marched up to Victoria, about 4 miles. Saw Dr. Evans and Mr Lucas. Wrote to Squire Sheffield and my sister. Slept in our tent for the first time. May 8th. Took rheumatism and had to give up the mines." But by mid-April, Evans had made his way to Yale where he became a merchant and bookkeeper for the Barnard's Express. While he went on to become Barnard's principal business manager, it is not known whether or not his rheumatism continued as a lifelong problem!

A traveller on the Cariboo road noted: "The stagecoaches were the aristocrats of the road. Traffic yielded to them and drivers entered and left stopping-places in a galloping flourish. The drivers were outstanding horsemen, able to drive for long hours in weather from scorching heat in summer to the 50 below zero of winter. Regardless of summer heat, mud and insects, or winter snow and blizzards, the schedule had to be maintained."

Once the Fraser's gold began running out, many miners pondered their futures. Some decided to go home. Others realized that British Columbia was a huge untapped wilderness with many potential sites for their personal *el dorado*. Some explored the Thompson River Valley and its streams before travelling further east. Most headed north, though, following the Fraser, and soon word leaked out that a new area promised riches beyond belief. American Watson Hodge was just one who saw his livelihood vanish with the Fraser's diminishing return. As he put it, "My whisky's gone, and credit too, / And I've put out for [the] Cariboo."

Since 1859 government officials and journalists had written about the area's "almost fabulous richness," with the Victoria *British Colonist* boasting that its sixty-four hundred square miles, a small area "fabulously rich in gold" could easily employ fifty thousand miners. For a while, it seemed the Cariboo might live up to such expectations. Once gold was discovered in Keithley Creek, men spread throughout the area. In September 1860 four prospectors discovered Antler

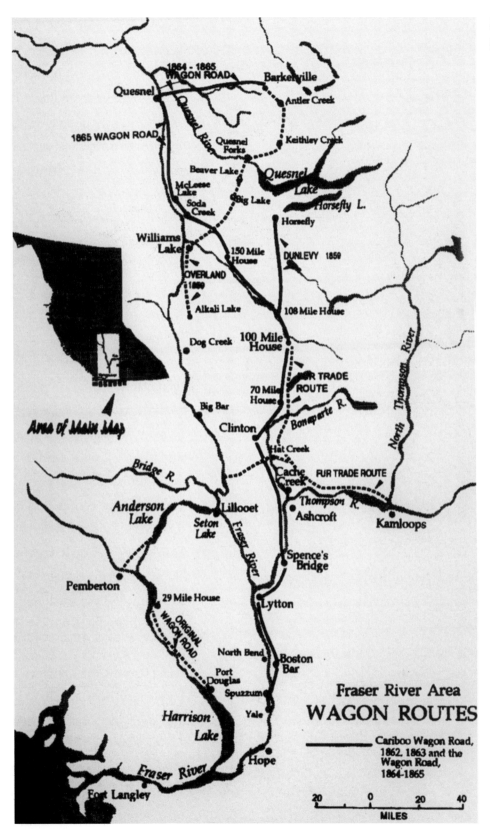

Map of the Fraser and Cariboo goldfields.

A handful of Cariboo gold.

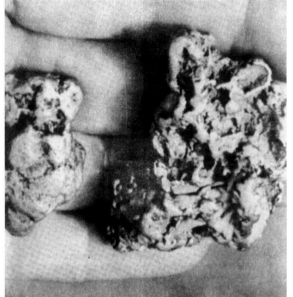

Frontispiece of *Cariboo, the Newly Discovered Gold Fields.*

CARIBOO,

THE NEWLY DISCOVERED

GOLD FIELDS

OF

BRITISH COLUMBIA,

FULLY DESCRIBED

BY A RETURNED DIGGER,

WHO HAS MADE HIS OWN FORTUNE THERE, AND ADVISES
OTHERS TO GO AND DO LIKEWISE.

"Men at these diggings get from three to ten ounces per day."—*See Times, February 5th, 1862.*

London:
PUBLISHED BY DARTON & CO., 58, HOLBORN HILL.

1862.

Creek, and within months the entire area had been staked out by miners who waited impatiently for the snow to thaw.

A Dutchman, William Dietz, was among them. After deciding to explore the surrounding area by snowshoe, he allegedly fell down a snowbank into the depression of a creek bed and, on a whim, pawed through the snow. When he opened his hand, he saw not only gravel but gold. Staking a claim immediately, he returned to Antler Creek and then travelled to Quesnel Forks for supplies. Unfortunately, he had not been able to hide his excitement. Prospectors traced his snowshoe tracks and, ignoring eight-foot mounds of snow, staked their claims.

The creek became the stuff of legends. Named Williams after Dietz it became one of the richest and most legendary of the gold-producing areas. Thomas Elwyn, the colony's gold commissioner, enthused that "the yield … on this creek is something almost incredible." During the previous three weeks, one company alone averaged two hundred ounces a day — which in 2003 would bring the owners more than US$700,000 daily. Elwyn continued, "These figures are so startling that I would be afraid to put them on paper, in a report for His Excellency's information, were I not on the spot and know them to be the absolute truth."

An ex-miner styling himself "A Returned Digger," wrote of his experiences in *Cariboo, the Newly Discovered Gold Fields.* Although many thousands of "Californian rowdies and

Australian diggers" swarmed throughout the colony, British readers should consider emigration. Fortunes were to be made. Using Antler Creek as an example, he told them that "raw hands" mined $200 daily and that one man's rocker had yielded $240 after ten hours' work. Two others regularly mined sixteen ounces a day. If they could do it, he implied, anyone could.

Other miners from the Cariboo began drifting back to Victoria on their way south to San Francisco, prompting more exuberant reports to Britain. In a letter to the Duke of Newcastle, Governor Douglas told of two men who arrived in the town "with nine thousand … dollars' worth of gold dust in their possession, being the fruits of three months' residence at the mines." Two others came to New Westminster, where Douglas personally inspected their treasure: "ten thousand dollars' worth of gold dust, the produce of five weeks' work at Cariboo." And in yet another letter the governor wrote that he "had not … met with a single unfortunate miner" from the region.

The *Daily Press* reported the effect of such reports on Victoria's residents in October 1861: "To say that our population have gone mad might be using an expression rather exaggerated. … Every person in the community is deeply infected with the gold fever and declares his intention at all hazards of leaving for Cariboo in the spring." Their excitement was easily understandable when Jones, for example, found that "Smith, who, not five months ago had not $200 in the world he could call his own, comes down from Cariboo heavily laden with $20,000 or $30,000 in gold."

Even the relatively staid *Times* of London published glowing reports of the seemingly endless supply of gold and the fortunes that could easily be accumulated. Its reporter in Victoria, Donald Fraser, told of five men who mined a fortune of $105,000 from a claim measuring eighty by twenty-five feet in two months. "There are no low earnings," Fraser assured his readers, and with reports such as these circulating throughout the world, another gold rush began. Men left wives and families, each believing they would become as wealthy as those they had read about. Many later

THOSE WHO OUGHT TO GO.

Capitalists, Artizans, Mechanics, Labourers and Able-bodied Men of every description.

Unmarried Females.

THOSE WHO OUGHT NOT TO .

Persons of a weak constitution, of no particular trade or calling.

YOUR HEALTH.

Beware of, and guard against yellow fever. Sulphate of quinine is a good, and in fact, the best preventative; next to that we must add personal cleanliness, i.e. frequent ablution, and do not be afraid of cold baths if you can get them, there is no fear of taking cold.

The symptoms of yellow fever are—headache, dry and burning skin, parched lips and dry mouth.

Champagne is the greatest enemy of yellow fever, and if you can afford to take half a dozen, do so, but it must be of good quality.

One ounce of quinine will be sufficient for the voyage; take 3 grains to form one dose daily, as a *preventative*. If attacked by the above symptoms, take 3 doses a day until it abates, if it should *not* abate then immediately consult the Doctor.

P. GRANT AND Co., Printers and Lithographers, 4, Red Lion Square, W.C.

"A Returned Digger's" advice for prospective emigrants.

Mount Baker as prospectors like W. Champness and George Blair would have seen it as they set out from New Westminster.

"The view of Harrison Lake is taken from a small bay ... about fifteen miles from Douglas ... In the distance are a portion of the Cascade Mountains and Mount Baker, an active volcano, situated in Washington Territory": *Illustrated London News.*

described their experiences in journals or books and from these accounts an entirely different picture of Cariboo gold mining emerged.

W. Champness was just one who left England for the Cariboo after reading such glowing accounts, and his observations and sketches would later be serialized in *The Leisure Hour*. He, together with George Blair from Upper Canada and John Sellars from Lower Canada, among others, painted a picture of unmitigated hell. For Champness, disillusionment began with his arrival in Victoria. As a bed was not to be found, he thought himself fortunate to sleep on top of a hotel's billiard table while others jostled for space on the floor. He travelled from Victoria to New Westminster by steamer, then transferred to the *Colonel Moody* for the trip to Port Douglas and the "generally adopted route to the upper country by a *detour* of lakes, rivers and portages."

W. Champness's impression of the much-maligned Port Douglas: "a wooden built town on a small lake. … But we need not thus specially characterize any one lake in British Columbia, for every lake, pond, stream, or valley hereabouts is embedded in mountains: the latter, like pine-trees and mosquitoes, are universal features and facts of the country."

At Port Douglas, Champness bought provisions and joined a party of prospectors for the long trek north. The first day they walked a disappointing total of eight miles, as the route was "exceedingly steep and rugged," but they pitched their tents beside a "clear mountain stream," ate a meal of bread, bacon, and tea, and slept relatively soundly, despite constant mosquito attacks. This first day would be a harbinger. The way would not become easier, the mosquitoes never quit, and the food rarely differed except for the addition of beans. Like Champness, Upper Canadian George Blair had taken the "easy" way to Victoria, sailing via Panama, boarding a train for the trip across the isthmus, thence to San Francisco by ship and transferring to yet another steamer for the final leg. He also chose to begin his trek to the goldfields at Port Douglas, carrying his own pack. But Blair complained about personal discomforts almost immediately. His feet became blistered after the first day and would remain a problem for the rest of the way. His sixty-pound pack (as opposed to the fifteen pounds that Champness carried) chafed his shoulders and all too soon they became "racked with pain."

Miners trekking to the goldfields with their backpacks. George Blair complained that his backpack chafed his shoulders until they became "racked with pain."

TRANSPORTATION TO THE CARIBOO — WEIRD, WILD, AND WACKY

With the astronomical cost of conveying goods to the Cariboo before the Royal Engineers built their road, various entrepreneurs tried to develop cheaper modes of transportation.

One of the simplest and least expensive was the trundle-wheelbarrow, which allowed a two-man team to transport about four hundred pounds of goods. The idea behind it was almost ridiculously simple — one man walked in front and would pull the wheelbarrow while his partner walked behind, pushing in the traditional way. Once developed, it provided miners an alternative to the back-breaking job of trekking along precipitous trails with sixty-pound packs on their backs.

The arrival of stern-wheeled steamers early in the gold rush period meant relatively safe transport. Flat-bottomed, they floated on top of the water and could operate in just a few inches of water. They could nudge up to a riverbank, then reverse course into the river. Experienced captains boasted they could "*walk* a steamer over a sandbar on its paddle wheel." Made of wood and extremely buoyant, they were easily repaired and could transport more than one hundred tons of freight. For decades they connected Victoria and Yale — a 185-mile trip — and also sailed between Soda Creek and Quesnel. Surprisingly impervious to the Fraser's ferocious rapids and white water, these utilitarian ships provided a lifeline to the Cariboo goldfields.

The trundle wheelbarrow.

The stern-wheeled steamer *Colonel Moody* on Soda Creek.

However, sternwheelers could not navigate their way through the Fraser Canyon and land transportation remained necessary. In 1862 a syndicate thought it would make its fortune by purchasing twenty-three camels in San Francisco from the U.S. government for three hundred dollars each. At first glance, the plan seemed sound. The animals could carry eight hundred pounds, travel thirty to forty miles a day, and go for days without food or water. British Columbia, though, would put a lie to those statistics, as any far-sighted person could have predicted.

Once the camels arrived, they promptly attacked everyone and everything in their vicinity. Accompanying this aggression was their pungent odour, which caused other pack animals to bolt. The owners tried to dispel the smell by washing the animals in scented water but their efforts were in vain and their workers had only bruises to show for their pains.

This did not douse some enthusiasm for them. In 1863 a Lillooet writer advised that the camels could "beat any transport we have, either ox, wagon, mule or cayoosh ponies. They are now acclimated and will eat anything from a pair of pants to a bar of soap." Miner Henry Guillod wrote that he was "bothered all day by the camels of which there are about a dozen here who have a neat idea of walking over your tent and eating your shirts."

Such habits, together with their smell and nasty dispositions, made the animals hated

The last of the camels, one of the more ill-advised money-making schemes.

throughout the Cariboo. Fortunately, and before they could be banned, it became obvious that the camels' days were numbered after they became footsore. Their hoofs, so good in sand, could not handle boulders, mud, or the Cariboo trail's rocky terrain. After a couple of years, the syndicate reluctantly turned some loose. At least one was slaughtered for meat, a few became tourist attractions, and one survived into the twentieth century.

While the camels were an "utter failure," they did at least transport some goods, unlike the wackiest of all the various ideas to improve transportation. F.J. Barnard and a partner, J.C. Beedy, imported four rubber-tired road steamers from Scotland. For weeks beforehand they proudly advertised their new mode of transportation, inviting people to "Steam to Cariboo!" Theoretically, each steamer could haul six tons of freight, and the first set off from Yale for the Cariboo in the spring of 1871 with great optimism. It reached Spuzzum that same day, Boston Bar the next, and Jackass Mountain on the third. And there the great experiment ended. The Scottish inventors had not envisioned British Columbian roads when they designed their steamers, and Barnard soon realized that his regular expresses were just as fast and, more importantly, less expensive and easier to maintain.

The camels kicked and bit horses and mules to death and it is impossible to declare which would have won if a camel train had encoun-

Advertisement for transportation in a Thomson Patent Road Steamer to the Cariboo.

tered one of the road steamers. But, in the general scheme of things, the camels may have had the last laugh. They at least had hauled freight for a couple of years from Yale to the Cariboo. Barnard's expensive experiment had quit after three days and after travelling only partway.

The more affluent, like Champness, hired horses, mules, and packers, who were frequently cruel. When the animals stumbled, the packers beat them unmercifully until stopped either by the animal's death or a miner's intervention. Champness described British Columbia as being "truly a horse-killing country" with rotting carcasses everywhere. One pack train started out with thirty mules but not one was alive by the time the men reached Antler Creek, "all having fallen … into the precipitous ravines … [where] sometimes a single stumble involves a fall of over a thousand feet." Sadly, he went on, the animals "do not die at once after falling, but linger awhile in horrible torture, far beyond the possibility of aid or access by their owners."

"We hired the services of an experienced Californian packer, who undertook to accompany us and securely pack our supplies on the beasts from time to time, at a uniform charge of thirty cents … per pound": W. Champness. Mules carried between 250 and 400 pounds and were not reined together in any way. Somehow each animal knew its place and kept it throughout long trips. An *aparejo*, a kind of leather sack filled with straw and lashed to the animal's back, replaced pack saddles.

Champness estimated that a mere 6 percent of those who left England for the goldfields actually arrived. Chance of success was therefore minuscule. But such odds could not deter the avid seeker. In manic eagerness the men set a blistering pace for the goldfields, frequently walking more than two hundred miles in sixteen days over difficult terrain. Between Williams and Beaver lakes, for example, Champness travelled through a region "where, for the extent of many miles, the earth was covered with innumerable thousands of dead and fallen trees, lying across each other in inex-

"The earth was covered with innumerable thousands of dead and fallen trees…": W. Champness.

Backpacking miners inching their way across a stream.

tricable confusion … whilst myriads of others were still standing, but leafless, dead and bleached, almost as white as snow." It was, he concluded, "as if Nature had set her curse" on the area. At least they could climb over them or inch their way along the trees. But if they slipped, they sank into a thick, black swamp and had to be helped out.

As Champness and his party trekked further north, they met large numbers of "poor, broken-down fellows" travelling in the opposite direction. Their "pale, pinched faces and tattered rags," he wrote, spoke eloquently "of hunger and poverty [and] were enough to dishearten all of us

together, for hundreds of such passed us during our journey." Seven of his group quit after hearing tales of unvarying disappointment, but Champness himself, like so many others, had gold fever. Logic, experience, and personal stories of disappointment could not prevail over the hope of staking a claim that would provide a monstrous fortune. Although tempted to despair, he felt that as he was "almost in the land of … [his hopes, he] would rather leave his bones there than abandon" his goal of reaching the Cariboo.

For those who travelled overland from Eastern Canada, conditions were equally as desolating. John Sellars left Huntingdon, Canada East

Before and after. Champness and his party passed "one [miner] who looked as if he had lain down to die, being pale, emaciated, worn out, and without a blanket or any covering but a few old rags. We were ourselves so scantily furnished with provisions that we were unable to render him much service. He made no complaint, and asked no relief; knowing well, as every one in this country does, that as a rule, travelling miners are unable to do more than grapple with their own troubles. But where they are able to help one another, the miners are a very generous set of men…": W. Champness.

Such despair helps explain the prevalence of "drink-shops" such as these along the Cariboo road.

(Quebec), in April 1862, with forty-eight other men "bound for British Columbia." Their departure had a party-like atmosphere, with "rabbelling" toasts to Britain and "hearty Cheers" for their homes and "Canada's Sons." At first, the way seemed easy. Trains took

Miners at a wayside inn. Champness observed that most "of the up-country whiskey is well vitrioled, and almost makes one's throat raw … Each person helps himself to as much as he pleases, without measure, merely pouring into a tumbler from the spirit-bottle at the bar."

them to Toronto, thence to Detroit, Chicago, and Fort Garry (Winnipeg). There they began their overland trek to Edmonton and the Cariboo. By August, a very lonely Sellars concluded that "starvation must be the fate of many of us long e'er we reach the Civilized World on the other side of the [Rocky] mountains." Every day seemed to bring "new trouble and trials not easy to be endured." He well remembered and bitterly regretted kissing his wife goodbye: "When we two parted, In silence and tears / Half broken hearted, To sever for years," and as they trekked mile after mile, he and other Overlanders constantly worried about running out of both food and money.

Catherine Schubert had one other worry. Together with her three small children, she accompanied her husband to the goldfields, one of only a few women to do so. For four months she endured the hardships of the trail, eating moss boiled with water when there was no other food, but something else made her situation unique: she was pregnant. And yet, such was the Overlanders' certainty that a fortune in gold awaited them that they kept going — at least as far as Quesnel Forks.

This town, fifty miles south of Antler Creek, was the main provisioning depot and news centre for the gold region. Champness described it as consisting of "general stores … and drinking shops" and being "prettily situated." Storekeepers eagerly welcomed newcomers, particularly if they had decided to give up and auction off whatever supplies and equipment they still had. Scores of defeated men helped such decision-making, telling tale after dis-

The intrepid Catherine Schubert.

couraging tale and bemoaning the fact that they had believed "the utter fallaciousness of certain writers who have sent home glowing reports of this land and its advantages." Thousands of them, according to Champness, "bitterly rued the day that they ever landed here," although Sellar offered the qualification that "an odd one now and then had done well." Even in the face of such reports, Champness, Blair, and Sellar did not turn back but compulsively pushed on towards Antler and Williams creeks and further disillusion.

The Schuberts' journey continued to be eventful. Catherine almost drowned when her canoe was smashed to pieces, survived several white-water rafting experiences, and must have been overwhelmed with joy when she sighted Fort Kamloops on the forks of the Thompson River. There, in a tent, she gave birth to her daughter Rose. Later, she would reflect that the end result of her trip was nothing but "hard work and no gold."

"A Returned Digger" was one of the writers who provided fallacious information. Gold, he exclaimed in his book, in the "Cariboo Diggings generally … is found near the surface — a few inches, a foot or two, and very seldom more than six feet" deep. That may have been the case when the first prospectors made their finds but by the summer of 1862 it was an entirely different story. Mining in the Cariboo had become a very expensive and difficult process involving a heavy outlay of money and deep exploration.

The hydraulic method of mining as explained by a mining handbook.

HYDRAULIC MINING.   271

boxes, generally 14 inches in length by about 3 feet in width. These are fastened together at the ends, and form a long and strongly built trough, extended as far as may be necessary—sometimes thousands of feet. It is lined with thick wooden blocks, partly to resist the friction occasioned by the passage of the *débris*, and also to allow room for quicksilver in the interstices for attracting and

HYDRAULIC MINING.

detaining the gold. Sometimes the quicksilver is placed in riffles, fixed transversely upon each other. This massive and continuous line of boxes is constructed near the bank about to be attacked. It is obvious that to bring down millions of tons of earth with the ordinary appliances of manual labour would be a tedious and profitless task. Another flume is therefore prepared for the purpose of bringing water from a level so much higher

As well, miners had to understand the hydraulic method of mining, which used vast quantities of water and had been perfected in the Californian gold rush of 1849. Guidebooks explained the process, and men learned that to excavate the gold, large amounts of gravel and dirt had to be washed away. Therefore, prospectors invested in flumes (the Californian name for the long wooden conduits that brought water to the diggings), sluice boxes, and water wheels, and, to afford the equipment, they forged companies in which shares frequently sold for one thousand dollars.

Even being part of a partnership, though, could not guarantee success, as George Blair discovered. He had reached Williams Creek in June 1862 where he found the miners "very busy, sinking shafts, building flumes and digging races." In the more shallow diggings they made

Hydraulic mining in practice.

"a stream of water" to wash away all the loose dirt of the topsoil. The remainder was shifted through sluice boxes, "a long string of troughs about a foot wide and ten inches high set on an incline" so that the water raced through them, leaving the pay dirt behind. Blair joined the "Never Sweat" and the "Bruce" mining companies but never managed to strike it rich and finally abandoned his search for gold in late 1863.

The Ne'er do Well mine dump, Grouse Creek.

The water wheel of the Alturas Gold Mining Company. Note the women in the background.

Illustration of a windlass and miners washing for gold.

The shaft entrance to the Never Sweat Tunnel Company claim, where Sellar worked briefly.

Sellar and Champness tried their luck for a mere two weeks or so before giving up. As Champness wrote resignedly in July 1862, "Gold was evidently around and beneath us, abundantly; but there seemed little or no hope of our being more fortunate in obtaining it than the majority of other miners. So ... after mutual deliberation and calculation, we resolved to do what multitudes had done before us — turn back again ... and sorely disappointed ... we began to retrace our steps over the same fatiguing route by which we had arrived." Ironically, they left before new discoveries turned Billy Barker and John Cameron into household names.

Billy Barker.

Billy Barker, a Cornish sailor, deserted his ship to follow the siren's call to the goldfields. After arriving in the Williams Creek area in August 1862, he staked his claim, constructed a shafthouse, and with a few others began digging. Allegedly inspired by a dream that promised him "pay at fifty-two," they dug down to fifty-two feet. What happened next gave a new definition to the

The windlass at the Barker claim. Billy is the bearded miner at the extreme right of the picture.

term *pay dirt*. The next shovelful of gravel was worth $1,000, which in 1860s monetary terms represented one-third of Begbie's annual salary. Billy Barker's share in this *el dorado* would eventually reach $650,000.

Miners who had previously dismissed him as a crackpot and laughed at his mine's location now rushed to stake the surrounding area, fighting off interlopers and each other. Friend turned against friend in the rush to share in Barker's fortune. Others built a shantytown with one narrow eighteen-foot street and named it Barkerville. Saloon keepers and other merchants flooded the area, cashing in on the seemingly endless bonanza and, in the long run, some proved smarter than Barker, who squandered his enormous wealth and died a pauper.

Barkerville looking from the creek towards Bald Mountain.

John Cameron would also die penniless and brokenhearted. He had come to the Cariboo from Ontario, travelling via Panama. Like Catherine Schubert, Cameron's wife, Sophia, showed uncommon courage and accompanied him together with their fourteen-month-old daughter. Their story is tragic, for adversity struck soon after they arrived in Victoria when their baby died. They eventually arrived in the Williams Creek area just after Billy Barker had found his motherlode.

With Robert Stevenson, who had accompanied them from Victoria, and some new friends, Cameron staked his claim a few hundred yards below Barker's on the creek, and Sophia must have wondered about his sanity. Her husband went to work each day; each night he returned with no good news. When Sophia contracted typhoid fever in late October and died shortly afterwards, the small community felt it had been dealt a mortal blow. Before her death, though, she had begged her husband to take her body back to Ontario, not to bury her in a lonely grave in the country that had made her life and that of her baby forfeit to her husband's obsession with gold. She died after hearing John's reassurance that he would indeed bury her in Ontario.

Cruelly, two months later John Cameron made the second-largest find on Williams Creek. Although his share yielded $350,000,

John "Cariboo" Cameron.

The Cameron claim. Reputedly John Cameron is bearded man sitting in the front row (second from the left) and Stevenson is leaning against the post.

lasting wealth proved as elusive as happiness. Grief-stricken, he fulfilled his promise to Sophia, taking her body back to eastern Ontario. But the Cariboo had him firmly in its talons. When his investments failed, he returned to the Williams Creek area and became a sad figure slinging hash in a town where he'd once been king.

Another view of the Cameron claim. Dr. Walter Cheadle wrote that after being treated to brandy and water, he and Lord Milton were taken down the thirty-foot shaft and found "numerous shafts all supported by timber & very closely roofed in with flat crosspieces. Wet, damp, dark & gloomy … They kindly helped us to wash out two pans which yielded some beautiful gold to the value of $21, nearly 1 1/3rd oz., we could see the nuggets lying in the gravel before loosened out by the pick!" They were shown "$1000 of gold in a bag, & the Company's books, showing weekly expenses averaging 7000 dollars … the yield being $29,000 per week!"

John Cameron's grave in the Barkerville area.

Another sense of the feverish activity on Williams Creek comes from the journal of Walter B. Cheadle, written in 1863. Cheadle did not have gold fever. Acting as a tutor to a young English nobleman, Lord Milton, he visited Canada as part of the young nobleman's education. Travelling overland from Eastern Canada, it seemed not even Milton's wealth and connections could ensure an easy trip, for they arrived in British Columbia in threadbare clothes and with almost no money. After refitting and recuperating in Victoria, they visited the Williams Creek area as tourists. "At dusk we arrived at Richfield," Cheadle later recalled, "the first part where gold was struck on this creek … It was quite dark before we reached Cameron Town below, passing

Walter Cheadle, tourist and tutor to Lord Milton, author of *The North-West Passage by Land*.

tho' Barkerville or Middle town. The whole 3 towns extending almost continuously down the creek for a mile and containing about 60 or 70 houses a piece." After pointing out that there had been only three or four houses before Cameron's success, he went on: "Our path was a difficult one over endless sluices, flumes and ditches, across icy planks and logs, all getting tumbles, gumboots being treacherous."

Barkerville. Cheadle noted that their path through it was "a difficult one over endless sluices, flumes and ditches, across icy planks and logs, all getting tumbles."

Richfield, showing the courthouse, magistrate's residence, and judge's residence.

One of Barkerville's more famous buildings. The hotel reputedly cost more than $10,000 to build.

Ironically, the fortunes of the three towns on Williams Creek would differ as dramatically as those of the three men responsible for their founding. Richfield, built near William Dietz's strike, became the centre of government in the area. Eventually, though, it would become, like Camerontown, a ghost town. Barkerville, almost immediately after Barker's success, became the miners' playpen. Although it was a mere collection of wooden buildings straddling one narrow street, the tiny town boasted that it was the largest city west of Chicago and north of San Francisco. It was certainly the largest "city" built on stilts in that expanse. The stilts protected residents

The famous narrow street of Barkerville (with the "ghost" dog).

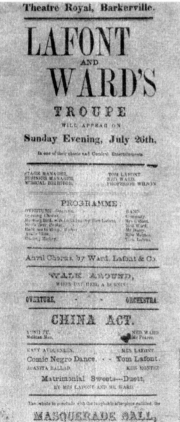

against mud and, more importantly, the buildings from the spring run-off. Barkerville supplied all the miners' needs with its barbers, druggists, tailors, theatre, churches, bakers, blacksmiths, shoemakers, two banks, two photographers, a Masonic lodge, and at least ten saloons.

Left: The program from a performance at Barkerville's theatre.

Right: J.H. Todd's store and the Wake-Up Jake Saloon, Barkerville.

Saloons were the most prevalent buildings throughout the goldfields, except for miners' shacks, of course. In them, men collected mail before frequently drinking their day's earnings, the unlucky consoled themselves while looking for work, and everyone exchanged news and gossip. An enterprising man might set up a saloon in his tent or a nearby cave and, provided there was liquor, prospectors would flock in after sundown. Barkerville's saloons, though, were the class of the Cariboo, for they featured the fabled dancing girls.

Miners at a wayside inn. Cheadle could not contain his disgust at certain establishments, calling one a "wretched place, no fire, no beds. Milton slept under the counter, I alongside it. Hall on top; 4 or 5 miners along the floor." Champness wrote similarly: "We were very crowded, as the small building was filled with miners by day and night, sleeping under the table and benches as well as on top of them, and all over the floor. Miners, in these parts and elsewhere, become so accustomed to their rough way of life, as to prefer sleeping on a floor, or even on the bare ground, if only dry, rather than in a soft bed.

Originally from Germany, the hurdy-gurdy girls had been part of the Californian goldfields, and, like many forty-niners, had simply moved north with the new gold rush. Their name derived from the hurdy-gurdy, a stringed instrument, but in Barkerville most of them danced to a fiddle. Lonely miners willingly paid one dollar for the chance to dance with them and were subsequently enticed into buying watered-down drinks. Once again, fortunes earned during the day were squandered at night. The enormously popular "dancing gals of the Cariboo" were not prostitutes. While most travelled to warmer climates during the winter, some married merchants and miners and lived year-round in the Williams Creek area. A ballad describes their philosophy: "Before we either give our hearts, / Or yet our sympath-ee, / You must be like this dear young man, / Who spends his all on me!"

Barkerville's famous hurdy-gurdy dancing girls.

The scarcity of women was a prevailing problem. As the "Returned Digger" wrote, "men stand up to look at a woman go past." In his experience, "the arrival of a fresh female face in a gold digging district created such a stir that the miners … knocked off work for the day, and had a kind of here and there meeting over the event." A *Times* correspondent put the situation more bluntly, "plain, fat and 50, even, would not be objected to; while good-looking girls would be … [like] nuggets." Encouraged by such reports, a "bride ship," sponsored by the British Female Emigration Society arrived in Victoria from England but the "mostly-clean, well-built" women married before they could embark on the four-hundred-mile trek to the Cariboo.

The hurdy-gurdy.

Contrary to popular opinion, the majority of women in the goldfields were married. The organized prostitution of the Californian diggings did not travel north. In fact, according to the *British Colonist*, nine American prostitutes caused a sensation when they arrived in the Williams Creek area. Dressed in "male attire," they swaggered "through the saloons and mining camps with cigars or huge quids of tobacco in their mouths, cursing and swearing." A revolver or bowie knife attached to their waist thoroughly dispelled any image of femininity, even for the female-starved miners. In general, only Native and Chinese women were sexually exploited and such exploitation was rarely organized. Some miners used liquor to entice Native women into their beds and procurers established a few Chinese brothels.

While the Cariboo lacked the legislative hostility and cut-throat atmosphere of the Californian goldfields, it was not free from prejudice. One claim, the Nigger, was called quite bluntly after the skin colour of those who mined it, and the "Returned Digger" offered this advice: "Take care whom you will sell your gold to. The Jews will be up at Frazer's River … and they will try all their usual games on you." Champness reported similarly, and George Blair, who used Biblical phraseology fondly, described his first sighting of Chinese miners: "We saw a gold-washing for the first time. Chinamen were ground sluicing on the banks of the river … [which] is [as] infested with Chinamen as the rivers of Egypt were with frogs."

THE CHINESE

British Columbia's first Chinese immigrants arrived among the thousands of other miners lured north by the shout of "Gold on the Frazer!" Some, who had been part of the Californian and Australian diggings, now sought this new opportunity to make their fortunes. Almost all, though, seized this chance to escape from California, where heavy taxes and restrictive immigration laws made their lives difficult.

In British Columbia, they faced the same suspicion and resentment amongst miners that they had sought to escape. Profound cultural, linguistic, and physical differences certainly contributed to this discrimination, but there were other factors. Many prospectors resented the Chinese habit of sending their capital back to China, rather than spending it locally. As well, their willingness to work for low wages meant that while employers appreciated them, their fellow workers despised them.

However, during the B.C. gold rush years, there were no repetitions of the ugly violence that had frequently erupted in California. The Chinese enjoyed a sense of safety despite the petty afflictions. Chief Justice Matthew Begbie boasted to a friend that in British Columbia "alone of all the mining countries will you find Chinamen, not protected, but standing in need of no protection [and] unmolested." Indeed, the law protected the rights of the Chinese miners and did so from the beginning when miners blockaded one of the first

Chinese prospectors working a bar on the lower Fraser. Note the rocker at the extreme right.

Staff cooks at Government House, New Westminster.

steamers to arrive because it carried Chinese passengers. Firm action by HBC Chief Trader Donald McLean ensured their safe landing and passage to Fort Langley, where they camped within the stockade's protection.

Once established, the Chinese thrived but never forgot the treatment they had endured in California. Bishop George Hills reported that when he reached a bridge at Ensley's Creek on his travels, where the toll was twenty-five cents for foot passengers and a dollar for a mule or horse, Ah Fat, the man in charge, refused to charge him. Apparently, the previous owner, an American, had charged high fees and "when the poor Chinamen came with no money, he would take away their mining implements." The local magistrate told them to build their own bridge. The result was an infinitely better one, and so they drove the American out of business. At a different bridge, another Chinese greeted Hills "with cool water to drink and told us we [would cross] free. ... No Englishman, he said, pays [to go] over the bridge, and no poor Chinaman. 'Me chargee Boston [American] man. Boston man chargee Chinaman very high in Californy. Chinaman now chargee Boston man, ha, ha'."

In general, though, the miners' animosity discouraged the Chinese from working the major diggings and they tended to mine only abandoned or marginal claims. During the Cariboo rush, the miners kept the Chinese out of Barkerville until their practice of patiently working abandoned claims eroded this prejudice and allowed them to participate in the life of the town. There, as was frequently the case, they quietly set up businesses, worked as cooks and launderers, helped develop the land by creating market gardens, and laboured on government projects such as the Cariboo road and, later, the Canadian Pacific Railway.

Sadly, their story does not have a happy end, as restrictive legislation was passed in 1885 when Parliament imposed a headtax of fifty dollars "on each and every Chinaman or Chinawoman [sic], every Chinese boy or girl landing in or coming into the province of British Columbia." They would be more popular, according to Sir Matthew Begbie, if they were "less industrious and economical, [and] if they would but occasionally get drunk, they would no longer be the formidable competitors with the white men which they prove to be in the labour market."

During the late 1850s and the 1860s though, British Columbian officials had ensured there was no official prejudice. In the context of the world as it was then, that truly was a magical achievement.

Doubtless Blair would have conjured up some Biblical allusion to describe "the Great Fire" that broke out in Barkerville on September 16, 1868, but he had long since returned home to Kincardine, Ontario. However, Frederick Dally, the photographer of approximately half the pictures in this book, described the town's destruction. The night before, while watching "the grandeur of the Aurora Borealis," his attention had wandered to the town "where dancing and revelry was going on." Stovepipes, which jutted "through the wooden roofs of the buildings at every height and in every direction," sent out "myriads of sparks and numbers of them" alighted on neighbouring houses.

When he mentioned his fears that a fire might easily break out to various businessmen the following morning, they told him the wood used to build the town was "different to other wood, and that it would not burn, otherwise the town would have been burnt [down] long since." Hours later, however, he "beheld a column of smoke rising from the roof of the saloon adjoining the stewards [sic] house." Apparently the fire began when a miner tried to kiss one of the hurdy-gurdy girls who was ironing in Barry & Adler's Saloon. Rebuffed, pushed back against a stove, he displaced its chimney and the canvas roof caught fire.

After collecting as many of his supplies as possible and depositing them in the middle of Williams Creek, Dally returned "certain that the town would be destroyed." The fire spread quickly, travelling "up and down the sides of the street, and as fast against the wind as it did before it." Although his building "was nearly fifty yards away from where the fire originated, in less than twenty minutes, it

An account of the Barkerville fire from the *Cariboo Sentinel*. Note that the Hudson Bay Company lost $65,000; Dally, the photographer, $1,100; and sundry "China houses" on the east side of the street more than $6,000, with one merchant, C. Strouss, losing $100,000.

Right: Barkerville, the morning after the fire.

together with the whole of the lower part of the town was a sheet of fire, hissing, crackling, and roaring furiously." Within an hour, the whole town was in flames.

Although rebuilding began at ten the following morning, the fire signalled both Barkerville's eventual demise and that of the Cariboo gold rush as well. The days of the "lucky" strikes were long gone, and mining now needed huge amounts of capital. Prospectors became employees, not casual workers — as in the early days when they might work to stave off starvation. The

The rebuilt Barkerville in 1868.

plight of many miners who did not strike it rich was almost beyond imagination. Far too many sacrificed everything in their conviction that they would be the one to find the motherlode. As their supplies, energy, and hopes dwindled, they found themselves trapped. After failing to find gold, "the one thing for which they bear to live," they could not find work and they could not afford food. Many simply gave up and walked into the woods to die solitary deaths. To heap ignominy on tragedy, few cared and relatives were rarely contacted, for many men were known only by their nicknames.

Others, equally desperate, chose to fight. In 1863 British Columbia had its first labour strife when Cariboo miners went on strike demanding to have their ten-hour shifts reduced to eight

Gloomy mining news from the *Cariboo Sentinel*: "It may safely be said that mining in Cariboo at present is at a standstill."

Right: Captain John Grant, senior officer of the Columbia detachment.

MINING INTELLIGENCE.

It may safely be said that mining in Cariboo at present is at a standstill. Nearly every creek is dried up, and the principal work that is being done in mining is in the prospecting or repairing line. There are eight claims on

WILLIAM CREEK

doing a little in the way of washing, viz.: The Barker, Sheepshead, Eagle, Sheepskin, Baldhead, Welsh, Lillooet, and Cariboo; and the whole amount taken out does not exceed 150 oz. On

MOSQUITO CREEK

the Minnehaha, Willow, Hocking, Point, Tabb and Discovery cos. are doing a little. The whole amount of gold taken out for the past week is about 350 oz. On

RED GULCH

the Catch-It, Butcher, United and Tom and Jerry cos. are making wages.

The only other creek we hear from that is washing is

CUNNINGHAM CREEK.

Sharp & co. have stopped hydraulicing and on Monday commenced to wash up for the season. It will take about two weeks to clean-up their ground sluice, and they estimate that they will have about $7900 for their summer's work.

There have been within the last week some very favorable accounts of strikes being made in different localities on

GROUSE CREEK

The Hard-up co. have got a good prospect in what is believed to be the old channel. On

SLATE GULCH

a company of 8 interests have struck a good prospect. On

HARD SCRABBLE CREEK

a fine prospect was struck on Friday last, in a blind shaft from the tunnel. This is looked upon as the best discovery that has been made for the season, as the creek is

An impressed Bishop Hills described their work. The Royal Engineers, he enthused, had changed the natural "tangled, rugged, pathless forest" into "a beautiful road upon which you might canter a coach." Such a beautiful road, though, had

hours and the pay raised from ten dollars to twelve. The mine owners agreed to this but then attempted to divide the men by attacking their leaders. When nothing worked, they successfully locked the workers out, forced them to accept the old pay rates and hours, then blacklisted the leaders throughout the colony until "all the bad and troublesome" men had been "gradually weeded out." In the short term the owners won — but the legacy of worker distrust would outlast the memories of the gold rush.

Therefore, it must have seemed another stroke of irony that a new wagon trail to the Cariboo guaranteed plentiful and relatively inexpensive supplies. Acting on Governor Douglas's orders, the Royal Engineers had begun building an eighteen-foot-wide road through the Fraser Canyon in the spring of 1862. The road was a work of genius, and a particular genius at that. Its primary engineer, John Marshall Grant, was a genius of construction — as the road proved.

required ingenious building techniques. First, the engineers solved the problem of the Harrison River's junction with the Fraser and the resulting silt by devising a series of cedar pilings and underwater bulwarks to force the river into a narrow channel where it scoured itself clean. One unfortunate sapper named Sturtbridge became so numb as he supported the pilings being pounded into the riverbed that he had to be pulled from the river. And while Lieutenant Mayne might joke that this was a "moist occupation," officials later complained about the size of Sturtbridge's medical bills after he developed rheumatism.

Other men hacked paths through rock faces and made cribbing from logs to buttress the road through crevices and ravines. One sapper froze to death while building a pier in a remote lake, and gangs of workers were hired to help build the road through treacherous precipices and ravines.

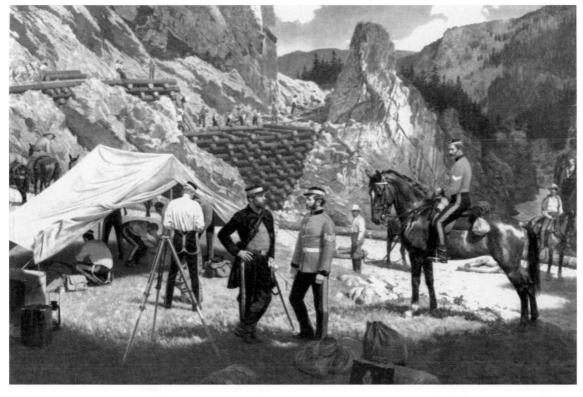

Labourers making the cribbing.

As the engineers blasted a way from Yale to Spuzzum, private contractors commenced work on other parts of the road. Joseph Trutch opened his Alexandra suspension bridge in September 1863, defraying his costs by charging a toll of $7.40 per ton. In relatively short order, the engineers completed the road through to Soda Creek, where traffic transferred to sternwheelers for the trip to Quesnel. The next section, Quesnel to Cottonwood, opened in 1864, and the road reached Williams Creek a year later. Wagon trains and stagecoaches took advantage of the new road and eventually Barnard's Express had a near monopoly on passengers.

The finished road showing the cribbing.

As described above, the road and its building sounds prosaic. However, it was anything but. Parts were hewn out of solid rock and the trail wound its way over paths that self-respecting mountain goats avoided. An animal's misstep now would not inevitably mean agonizing death, and British Columbians proudly described the road as "the eighth wonder of the world," fully expecting that sections of the engineers' masterpiece would last forever.

Hotels and way-houses opened up along the route at ten to fifteen mile intervals, though sometimes a mere three or four miles apart. Usually they offered Spartan accommodation, and cleanliness was not considered a virtue by many of those who ran them. Numerous stories

A stretch of the road where the Royal Engineers carved the road from rock. While Champness watched the blasting, he "heard a rushing noise, and, looking up, saw a large body coming down headlong from the elevated trail. It proved to be a splendid mule, which had made a false step and so fallen headlong."

were told of newcomers whose request for a clean spoon would send all others into fits of laughter. Some hotels advertised the cleanliness of their stables rather than their beds. Others had extremely low standards, as Dr. Cheadle found out: "The wind blew thru cracks in walls and floor, only one blanket apiece, 20 men in the room … one swearing every half hour."

In Clinton, the main hotel was run by Mrs. Tom Marshall, described as being rough and ready by nature and a woman who not only swore and smoked but lit her matches on the soles of her shoes. However, Mrs. Sarah Crease, who travelled extensively throughout the interior of British

Sir Joseph Trutch, who became a powerful influence in the shaping of British Columbia.

Trutch's Alexandra suspension bridge.

The Colonial Hotel at Soda Creek

Left: Advertisements for various hotels and way-houses on the Cariboo road from the *Cariboo Sentinel*, including the Clinton Hotel.

Right: The Clinton Hotel, one of the few establishments granted Mrs. Sarah Crease's approval.

Columbia and was the "Martha Stewart" of her time, gave Mrs. Marshall and her hotel top marks — a departure from her usual scathing criticism. After a "lovely drive" into Clinton, Crease wrote, they arrived at "Mrs. Marshall's … cold and tired. House very clean and comfortable. Mrs. Marshall an honest talking, rough, kind hearted woman. Food very good, delicious butter and cream, bed soft and comfortable. Breakfasted on delicious oatmeal porridge and cream. At lunch Mrs. Marshall brought me a plate of soup and entertained me with an hour's gossip about herself and her neighbours." Maybe Mrs. Crease would not have been quite so entertained if she could have heard the gossip about herself in the following days.

Sarah Crease, wife of Henry Pering Pellew Crease.

The discovery of gold on the Fraser and in the Cariboo irrevocably changed British Columbia and, for a long time, many must have wondered if any lasting good would come to the new colony. The decline began before the Barkerville fire, although that epitomized the many dreams that went up in smoke. Newspaper advertisements in 1868

Faced with the collapse of mining in Camerontown, the owner of the Pioneer Hotel moved her establishment to Mosquito Creek.

tell the story. The Richfield hotel was for sale, and way-houses and hotels along the Cariboo route offered cut-rate prices on both bed and board.

As disappointed miners and prospectors trudged their way south, they left behind profound ecological damage. In their haste to build flumes and sluices, they had ravaged the forests and the river systems. Williams Creek was just one treated "in the most ignominious manner," wrote Byron Johnson. "A little above the town [Barkerville] it flowed along silvery and clear as it had been wont to do; but soon inroads were made upon its volume in the shape of ditches cut from it, and continued along the sides of the hills, to feed the huge overshot waterwheels that appeared in all directions."

Williams Creek winding its way through the desolated landscape towards Barkerville in the distance.

After describing the "dirty streams [which] were poured forth by the sluices," Johnson described other ecological damage. "From the hills," he wrote, "came the perpetual cracking and thudding of axes, intermingling with the crash of falling trees, and the grating undertone of the saws as they fashioned the logs into planks and boards. From the bottom of the valley rose the splashing and creaking of waterwheels, the grating of shovels, the din of the blacksmith's hammer sharpening pickaxes." All this activity, though, turned to naught. Towns like Richfield, which had been proud symbols of lucky strikes, began their slow decay into ghosts of the past.

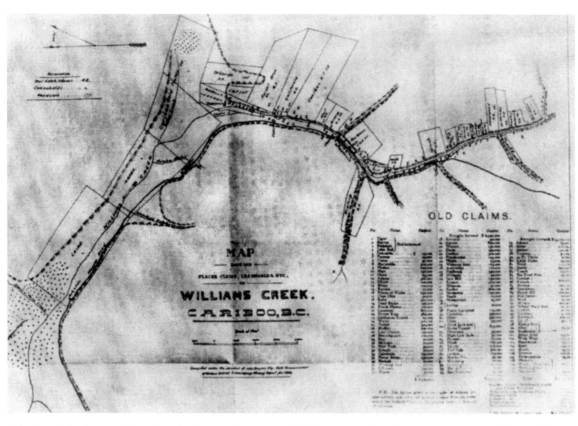

A survey showing the multiplicity of claims along Williams Creek.

The wealth dug so laboriously from the ground did not stay in the area — most of it ended up in the United States.

Even more devastating was the impact the miners and their rush for gold had on the various Native peoples. Ecological destruction changed ancestral hunting patterns, and centuries-old nomadic habits altered as first miners and then settlers moved into their lands. The most profound tragedy, however, came following the arrival in Victoria of a sick would-be miner from San Francisco in March 1862.

Once he was diagnosed with smallpox, the ramifications of his disease became quickly apparent. At least two thousand northern Natives had decided to move south for the winter to trade with the seasonal influx of miners in Victoria. Almost immediately the *British Colonist* worried about the "fearful calamity" if the "Indians on the outskirts of the town" were to catch the disease. Events soon proved the newspaper's worry true. The disease spread through the Native communities faster than attempts to contain it. Dr. John Helmcken vaccinated as many as he could — several hundred in the first few weeks — but the pox seemed manically obsessed with propagating itself. It was as though two highly contagious diseases had arrived almost simultaneously: smallpox, which would devastate the First Nations, and gold fever, which also destroyed thousands upon thousands of lives.

A First Nations mask vividly depicting the horror of smallpox. Like almost every other commentator, Champness wrote about the effects of the disease. "The dread … far surpasses their fear of violent or sudden death. The manner in which the sick and dying are thus forsaken by their companions is merely one amongst numerous illustrations of the degradation and depravity of human nature. … In the case of the abandoned Indians just referred to, they all died one after another, and remained unburied for days, until their bodies attracted the attention of some white neighbours."

Within weeks, the disease spread throughout Vancouver Island. A sailor noted twelve bodies "festering in the noonday sun" on a Nanaimo beach and a schooner captain reported the Natives' attempt to contain the illness: when the smallpox "pustules break out on an occupant on one of the canoes, he is put ashore; a small piece of muslin, to serve as a tent, is raised over him, a small allowance of bread, fish and water doled out and he is left to die alone." Then the canoes travelled away, with the paddlers unaware they might be infected as well.

Others did what they could. The chief trader at Kamloops vaccinated as many of the Shuswap people as possible; those who travelled around the colony took medicines and vaccinations with them, as Reverend John Sheepshanks described: "Sitting down upon a fallen tree and taking out my lancet, I told the chiefs that I wished to cut them all slightly on the arm and put in a little good medicine which I hoped — I tried to express myself carefully — would preserve them from the bad disease."

Despite such efforts, the devastation continued for another two years. Naturally the Natives blamed the Europeans for introducing the disease, which literally erased some villages and decimated others. Robert Stevenson (John Cameron's prosperous friend) recorded that he had "counted 90 snow graves of Indians who died here from the smallpox. There was only one adult Indian of the Beaver Lake tribe living. … At Williams Creek I counted 120 snow graves, and only three grown Indians left." Story after story reported the same stark picture. Faced with such tragedies, the Tsilhqot'in people fought a minor war after Alfred Waddington's up-country agent foolishly and callously threatened to "send sickness into the country" to kill them all.

He need not have worried. Smallpox was doing an extremely thorough job on its own as the following statistics show. In 1835, the Haida people numbered about 6,000. In 1885 their total had shrunk to 800 and would eventually reach its nadir of 588 in 1915, while the Kwakiutl population dropped from 10,700 in 1835 to 3,000 in 1885. These huge losses partially explain

Indian graves at Boston Bar. George Blair visited "an Indian burial ground … Waving on high flagstaffs were flags of every colour, some with crosses on them. On every bush and on sticks put up for the purpose were hanging old rags, pieces of blankets, baskets, wooden bowls, or dishes and moccasins."

why the various aboriginal people, weakened by smallpox, did not resist when settlers occupied their ancestral lands. As well, men with little or no experience in negotiating treaties had taken over the reins of government from Douglas. The consequent lack of treaties for most of British Columbia thus became a problem for twenty-first-century politicians to solve.

Other legacies from the gold rush were also long-lived. The Cariboo road, of which British Columbians were so justifiably proud, was an economic disaster. Ironically, the labour of the Royal Engineers created a massive debt (approximately $650,000 in 1863) and hope for the recovery of funds faded as rapidly as good news from the Cariboo.

As well, tension developed between the twin colonies of Vancouver Island and British Columbia because only the island profited from the latter's wealth. As B.C. Governor Frederick Seymour grumbled, "The merchants and owners of Town lots in Victoria in the comparatively unimportant Colony of V.I. have drawn nearly all the share of the profits of the gold discoveries in this Colony which have not been absorbed by California." Seymour's attempts to raise

In 1862 George Blair observed "carved images of bear, deer and some other animals I could not make out" on Native graves. A decade later the full effect of European settlement could be seen in this engraving from the *Canadian Illustrated News*. Representations of the family show it in European clothing standing watch over a grave on the Cariboo road below Lytton.

Europeanized totem poles, c. 1870.

Governor Seymour "gaming" on his way to British Columbia. This photograph was taken between Portland and Vancouver Island.

money by charging higher fees and import duties only plunged B.C. into deeper debt as its population began drifting away.

But not to Vancouver Island, which, despite its preferred status, was having its own financial crisis as rents tumbled and merchant after merchant went into bankruptcy. As well, the cost of running two colonies with dual, overlapping bureaucracies was ruinous — $954,000. Revenues rarely exceeded $210,000 and together the colonies had a combined debt of $1,296,681. To help reduce the costs, Seymour proposed an amalgamation, which London approved, although, he noted sourly, "There was no enthusiasm or excitement shown in either town." Ex-governor Douglas thought that a "funeral procession … would have been more appropriate to the sad melancholy event." Functions that had previously been the domain of Victoria now shifted to the mainland capital of New Westminster, which had seemingly outgrown its image as a "city of stumps" to become, in Seymour's words, "the most respectable, manly and enterprising little community" he had ever known.

He should have read an article on the city in the August 12, 1865 issue of *Harper's Weekly*. "The City of New Westminster is pleasantly situated on the north bank of the Fraser, about fifteen miles from its mouth," the magazine announced, before going on to say that at the time it

Victoria. "The government buildings, Supreme Court and the hall occupied by Parliament, form one pile of buildings, and are separated some distance from the chief thoroughfare of the town by James Bay": Matthew Mackie, *Vancouver Island and British Columbia.*

The illustration accompanying the *Harper's* article on New Westminster.

Columbia Street, New Westminster, c. 1868.

The mint and government bakery, 1862, New Westminster.

became British Columbia's capital in 1859, "a dense forest covered the present site of the city … Many of the stumps still remaining in the city, measure from 15 to 20 feet in diameter. [The trees] average over 200 feet in height, and one which was recently cut at New Westminster was 309 feet in height." Majestic trees indeed, but equally majestic stumps and these could not mitigate against the "civilized" facade of Victoria.

Another fight broke out about the location of the united colony's capital, with Dr. Helmcken a strong supporter of the previous capital. He served notice that he would fight Seymour about this in the first meeting of the new legislative council in New Westminster by introducing a resolution to move "the Seat of Government to Victoria." It made sense. Victoria was, by far, the largest city in the colony, the centre of commerce, and within walking distance of the British naval base at Esquimalt. Although Helmcken lost the first vote, he won the second, and Seymour sadly backed down and proclaimed Victoria the capital of the united colony of British Columbia.

According to the *Canadian Illustrated News*, Esquimalt afforded "the most perfect shelter to ships of large tonnage that can be obtained between this location and San Francisco… In this capacious place … a portion of H.M. Pacific squadron already rides; and eventually Esquimalt is certain to assume the position of chief depot for the Royal Navy in that area."

Such squabbles could not eclipse the massive and ever-accumulating debt, which for British Columbia's population was $163 per head. As more people recognized that the colony could not continue without radical change, residents began debating three solutions. The first was readily recognized as a long shot: the colony could remain British and ask London for funds to pay its debt. The second had widespread support.

A more "civilian" view of Esquimalt.

As debate swirled, two men observed the colony from a vastly different perspective. Lieutenant Colonel Robert Scott and Major James Hoyt of the U.S. Army came to the conclusion that the only salvation for British Columbia would be through annexation to the United States. Furthermore, they thought most residents agreed with them. They had considerable justification for this. In 1867 the personal taxation level had risen to $87.50. The cost of governing the eight thousand or so non-Native residents came to $64,000 — the same sum being spent to administer California's half-million inhabitants and six times the amount incurred to govern the neighbouring Washington territory. The Scott-Hoyt report painted a damning picture: "Victoria presents a melancholy spectacle of premature decay and financial ruin. Day after day we saw large wholesale trading establishments without a customer, the proprietors looking gloomily over their open ledgers in despair… Grass is literally growing in the thoroughfares formerly crowded with teams and busy drays." In their opinion, New Westminster had reverted to being a city of stumps: "We found the place nothing more than a small village built among the stumps of the forest."

Annexation was a feasible solution. Britain had no interest in paying off the colony's debt, particularly since the Crimean War had ended and the United States had bought Alaska from Russia in 1867. Annexation, therefore, would give American interests the entire northern Pacific coast. In addition, most of British Columbia's imports came from the United States, many residents originated from there, and influential people, such as the American consul in Victoria, were convinced that "the people of Vancouver Island and British Columbia are almost

Victoria. "Large and substantial stone and brick warehouses, well stocked with goods, line the upper part of the harbour on the town side. … Several spacious hotels, elegantly furnished, and supplied with every comfort which the most fastidious could wish, have been built." When Matthew Mackie wrote this description in 1865, he could not foresee that within a very short time weeds would grow in this thoroughfare and the spacious hotels would be empty.

unanimous in the desire for annexation to the United States." As well, American capital had symbolically made the colony an integral member of the wider world.

New Westminster became part of an "immense enterprise" in 1865 that planned to connect America to Europe by way of California, Oregon, Washington territory "under the auspices of the Western Union Telegraph Company." According to *Harper's Weekly*, the telegraph line would continue from New Westminster to the Bering Strait, thence through Siberia until it connected to the Russian government's telegraph lines.

The scope of this feat cannot be underestimated, nor can its effect on the fledgling colony. News from the eastern portion of the continent now reached New Westminster within hours instead of weeks. This meant that those who had come to British Columbia from British North America could follow the eastern debate about Confederation with some immediacy. As a result, another solution to the question of B.C.'s debt arose that almost no one had given thought to until a transplanted Nova Scotian named Amor De Cosmos raised the issue.

Born William Smith, De Cosmos had legally changed his name in California (though why a person capable of sudden and deep hatreds should imagine he was the lover of the world must remain a historical mystery). But in March 1867, at the same time London was finalizing the British North America Act, which would join Nova Scotia, New Brunswick,

The American flag waving proudly beside the building housing Collins Overland Telegraph in New Westminster.

and the Canadas (East and West) into a confederation, De Cosmos proposed that British Columbia join this new dominion. This idea took most of his fellow legislators by surprise as Dr. Helmcken admitted: "No one knew much about this subject save De Cosmos." The idea, though, gained immediate favour, and the council advised the governor to proceed "without delay ... to insure the admission of British Columbia into the Confederation on fair and equitable terms."

This resolution did not affect the pro-annexationists for they could not believe that Canada would be willing to assume the huge British Columbian debt. In December 1869 forty-three residents of Victoria petitioned Ulysses S. Grant, the U.S. president: "We earnestly desire the

The transplanted Nova Scotian William Smith who legally changed his name (in San Francisco) to Amor De Cosmos. He played an integral part in bringing British Columbia into Canada and became its second premier.

ACQUISITION of *this Colony* by the *United States.*" Although the *British Colonist*, published by Amor De Cosmos, scoffed that this "was a sublime bit of cheek," the public generally supported annexation. Until, that is, it learned of the incredible terms its new governor, Anthony Musgrave, intended to set as his basis for admission to Canada, and to achieve his goals he built a powerful coalition. Dr. Helmcken, although not initially favouring De Cosmos's idea, was appointed to the executive council, where he suggested B.C. demand a railway from the lower Fraser River area to Kamloops and a wagon road from there through the Rocky Mountains.

Trutch, the builder of the Alexandra suspension bridge, thought Helmcken had not been sufficiently audacious. "Helmcken," he exclaimed, "your ideas of a waggon road and a railroad are good but on thinking the matter over I think Confederation will be valueless without a railway to Eastern Canada."

"Heavens, Trutch," the doctor replied, "how are they to build it! — and as to operate it — I do not see the way!"

"Well I do," the bridge-builder replied.

To everyone's incredulity Canada agreed to British Columbia's terms, including the absorption of the crippling debt. But as late as May 1871 problems remained. Government officials, like Chief Justice Matthew Begbie, worried about their pensions, particularly with each negotiating his own terms. After one tedious session Governor Musgrave snapped, telling Begbie that he was "as difficult to satisfy as St. Thomas the Unbeliever." But eventually the problems sorted themselves out, and July 20, 1871, was set for the official date for admittance to Canada. As the

Government buildings in Victoria known as the "Birdcages."

clock wound down on their colonial past, people throughout British Columbia prepared to celebrate. All were proud of the "super-excellent" bargain their negotiators had made. Bunting adorned most buildings, flags waved happily in the breeze, and as midnight church bells carolled, fireworks exploded, and people in Victoria took to the streets and "cheered, and cheered, and cheered." The *British Colonist* reported this incident as "the Birth of Liberty."

Barkerville was no less enthusiastic, celebrating the day with gunfire salutes and the pealing of fire bells. Its future would be a rocky one. For years it fought valiantly against becoming a ghost town like Richfield and Camerontown until, in the 1950s, the Cariboo Historical Society petitioned the provincial government for restoration, claiming Barkerville as "the true birthplace of the province." Rescued from future oblivion, the town became a provincial park in 1958 and has thrived for years as a major tourist attraction.

An advertisement in the *British Colonist* for a celebratory picnic.

The ruins of "Cariboo" Cameron's cabin.

In the short term, the gold rush brought economic hard times. Unlike Australia and California, where the miners settled after slaking their thirst for gold, most of B.C.'s gold seekers returned to their homes, and it took many years before the population returned to the dizzying heights of the 1860s. As well, the ecological damage wrought by the miners took decades to repair and in some instances was permanent. The First Nations people also underwent permanent change. For them, there was no miraculous happy ending, and the gold rush meant only profound desolation. It must also be recognized that the manic search for gold cost tens of thousands of lives — First Nations, would-be miners, and the animals forced to carry their supplies.

Once the shout of "Gold on the Frazer!" was heard and answered worldwide, change became inevitable. The resource-rich wilderness of New Caledonia, where First Nations and Hudson's Bay employees coexisted amicably, changed overnight into the colony of British Columbia, a place where men driven by greed would plunder the land in their compulsive search for more gold. Victoria, once a placid fort, "a quiet village of 800 inhabitants," endured a frenetic building boom and economic depression to eventually become the capital of the province of British Columbia. New Westminster shone briefly before being eclipsed by the birth of a bigger, neighbouring city when the cross-continental railroad, negotiated as part of B.C.'s terms for joining Canada, spawned the city of Vancouver.

Would-be miner W. Champness wrote that British Columbia was "on the whole, very favourable to … emigrants" and predicted a time when "Divine wisdom" might draw from the "uttermost parts of the earth an enterprising and industrious population, who at no distant period [would] unite by railway and telegraph the commerce, the civilization … with the hitherto neglected and underdeveloped regions of the far North Pacific." He could not have foreseen the pluralism and diversity of 2003 British Columbia, yet his wish for it remains prescient: "one comprehensive union of enlightened intercourse and prosperity, both temporal and spiritual." If such could ever be achieved, it would indeed be the finest legacy from the Fraser and Cariboo gold rushes.

SELECTED BIBLIOGRAPHY

PRIMARY SOURCES

Archival:

Archives of British Columbia
Library and Archives of Canada
New Westminster City Museum
Online Archives of California
Special Collections, University of British Columbia

Contemporary Magazines and Newspapers:

British Colonist (and variants of the name)
Canadian Illustrated News
Cariboo Sentinel
Harper's Weekly (and *Monthly*)
Illustrated London News
Leisure Hour
Punch
Victoria Gazette

Contemporary Books and Guides:

Anderson, Alexander C. *Handbook and Map to the Gold Region of Frazer's and Thompson's Rivers.* San Francisco: J.J. LeCount, 1858.

Ballantyne, Robert M., ed. *Handbook to the New Gold Fields: A Full Account of the Richness and Extent of the Fraser and Thompson River Gold Mines.* Edinburgh: Alex Strahan, 1858.

Cheadle, Walter B. *Journal of a Trip Across Canada 1862-1863.* 1931. Reprint. Edmonton: Hurtig, 1971.

Cornwallis, Kinahan. *The New El Dorado; or British Columbia.* London: T.C. Newby, 1858.

Ham, Thomas. *The Gold Diggers Portfolio.* Melbourne: Cyrus Mason, 1854.

Hazlitt, William Carew. *The Great Gold Fields of Cariboo.* London: W. Penny, 1858

Higgins, David. *Mystic Spring, and Other Tales of Western Life.* Toronto: William Briggs, 1904.

Mayne, R.C. *Four Years in British Columbia and Vancouver Island.* London: J. Murray, 1862.

[A Returned Digger]. *Cariboo, the Newly Discovered Gold Fields.* London: Carton & Hodge, 1862.

Waddington, Alfred. *The Fraser Mines Vindicated, or The History of Four Months.* Victoria: P. DeGrarro, 1858.

SECONDARY SOURCES

Anderson, Gerald Smedley. *Sir Joseph William Trutch 1826-1904.* [Victoria]: B.C. Lands Service, 1972.

Baskerville, Peter A. *Beyond the Island: An Illustrated History of Victoria.* Burlington, Ont.: Windsor Publications, 1986.

DeVolpi, Charles P. *British Columbia: A Pictorial Record, Historical Prints and Illustrations of the Province of British Columbia Canada, 1779-1891.* Sherbrooke, Que.: Longman Canada, 1973.

Downs, Art. *Wagon Road North.* Surrey, B.C.: Foremost, 1973.

Goodman, David. *Gold Seeking: Victoria and California in the 1850s.* Stanford, Calif.: Stanford University Press, 1994.

Grant, Peter. *Victoria: A History in Photographs.* Vancouver: Altitude, 1995.

Griffin, Harold. *Radical Roots: The Shaping of British Columbia.* West Vancouver, B.C.: B. Griffin c. 1999.

Harris, Lorraine. *Barkerville: The Town that Gold Built.* Surrey, B.C.: Hancock, 1984.

Holliday, J.S. *The World Rushed In: The Californian Gold Rush Experience*. New York: Simon and Shuster, 1981.

Howay, F.W. *British Columbia: The Making of a Province*. Toronto: Ryerson, 1928.

Howay, F.W. *British Columbia from the Earliest Times to the Present*, Vol. 2. Vancouver: S.J. Clarke, 1914.

Keesing, Nancy, ed. *Gold Fever: Voices from Australian Goldfields*. New South Wales: Eden Paperbacks, 1967.

Laut, Agnes. *The Cariboo Trail, a Chronicle of the Gold-fields of British Columbia*. Toronto: Glasgow, Book & Company, 1922.

Molyneux, Geoffrey. *British Columbia: An Illustrated History*. Vancouver: Raincoast, 2002.

Morrell, W.P. *Gold Rushes*. New York: Macmillan, 1941.

Patenaude, C. Branwen. *Trails to Gold*. 2 vols. Victoria: Horsdal & Schubart, 1995.

Pearson, John. *Furs & Gold*. White Rock, B.C.: S.K. Press n.d.

Reksten, Terry. *The Illustrated History of British Columbia*. Vancouver/Toronto: Douglas & McIntyre, 2001.

Stangoe, Irene. *Cariboo-Chilcotin: Pioneer People and Places*. Surrey, B.C.: Heritage House, 1994.

Sterne, Netta. *Fraser Gold 1858: The Founding of British Columbia*. Pullman, Wash.: Washington State University Press, 1998.

Williams, David Ricardo. *The Man for a New Colony*. Sidney, B.C.: Gray's, 1977.

PHOTO CREDITS

Page 19:   Top: *Canadian Illustrated News,* 1872

Bottom: *Harper's Weekly,* 1858

Page 20:   Top: Bancroft Library, University of California, Berkeley BANC PIC 1973.002.0052

Bottom right: Latrobe Collection, State Library of Victoria, Australia

Bottom left: BC Archives, PDP 2612

Page 21:   Top left: Ham, Thomas. *The Gold Diggers Portfolio.* Melbourne: Cyrus Mason 1854

Top right: BC Archives, A-00353

Bottom left: *Leisure Hour,* 1865

Bottom right: *Canadian Illustrated News,* 1872

Page 22:   Top: BC Archives, A-01075

Bottom: from Patenaude, C. Branwen. *Trails to Gold.* 2 vols. Victoria: Horsdal & Schubart 1995, used with the permission of Heritage House Publishing

Page 23:   from Howay, *British Columbia,* vol. II

Page 24:   Top: *Illustrated London News,* 1864

Bottom left: *Illustrated London News,* 1864

Bottom right: *Illustrated London News,* 1864

Page 25:   Top: Special Collections, Baillieu Library University of Melbourne

Bottom: from Canadian Jackdaw, *Gold in the Cariboo*

Page 27:   Top: from Agnes C. Laut, *Cariboo Trial, A Chronicle of the Gold fields of British Columbia.* Toronto: Glasgow, Brook & Company 1922

Bottom: BC Archives, A-03885

Page 28:   Top left: BC Archives, A-01723

Top centre: BC Archives, A-01701

Top right: BC Archives, A-01625

Bottom: BC Archives, A-01886

Page 29: Top: from Mayne, R.C. *Four Years in British Columbia and Vancouver Island.*
London: J. Murray 1862
Bottom: from Howay, *British Columbia,* vol. 2

Page 30: Top: BC Archives, A-01127
Bottom: Laut, *Cariboo Trail*

Page 31: Top: BC Archives, B-04076
Bottom: Howay, *British Columbia,* vol. 2

Page 32: Top: BC Archives, A-02341
Bottom: BC Archives, G-05683

Page 33: Left: *British Colonist,* 1863
Right: BC Archives, C-03661

Page 34: Howay, *British Columbia, vol. 2*

Page 35 from Patenaude, C. Branwen. *Trails to Gold.* 2 vols. Victoria: Horsdal & Schubart
1995, used with the permission of Heritage House Publishing

Page 36: Top: from Downs, Art. *Wagon Road North.* Surrey, B.C.: Foremost 1973, used with
permission by Heritage House Publishing
Bottom: from *Cariboo: The Newly Discovered Fields*

Page 37: Ibid.

Page 38: Top: from Mayne, R.C. *Four Years in British Columbia and Vancouver Island.*
London: J. Murray 1862
Bottom: *Illustrated London News,* 1864

Page 39: *Leisure Hour,* 1865

Page 40: BC Archives, PDP 00017

Page 41:   Top: BC Archives, A-00556

                Bottom: Howay, *British Columbia*, vol. 2

Page 42:   BC Archives, A-00347

Page 43:   *British Colonist*, 1871

Page 45:   *Leisure Hour*, 1865

Page 46:   Top: *Leisure Hour*, 1865

                Bottom: *Leisure Hour*, 1865

Page 47:   Top: *Leisure Hour*, 1865

                Bottom: Howay, *British Columbia*

Page 48:   from Cheadle, Walter B. *Journal of a Trip Across Canada 1862-1863*

Page 49:   BC Archives, A-03081

Page 50:   Top: Canadian Jackdaw, *Gold in the Cariboo*

                Bottom: Howay, *British Columbia*, vol. 2

Page 51:   Top: National Archives of Canada, C-021575

                Bottom: National Archives of Canada, C-008078

Page 52:   Top: from Cheadle, Walter B. *Journal of a Trip Across Canada 1862-1863*

                Bottom: National Archives of Canada, C-000173

Page 53:   Top: BC Archives, A-01144

                Bottom: National Archives of Canada, C-019424

Page 54:   Howay, *British Columbia*, vol. 2

Page 55:   Top: Howay, *British Columbia*, vol. 2

Bottom: National Archives of Canada, C-088923

Page 56:   Top: Howay, *British Columbia*, vol. 2

Bottom: from Downs, Art. *Wagon Road North*. Surrey, B.C.: Foremost 1973. Used with permission of Heritage House Publishing.

Page 57:   Top: from Cheadle, Walter B. *Journal of a Trip Across Canada 1862-1863*

Bottom: National Archives of Canada, C-024479

Page 58:   Top: Howay, *British Columbia*, vol. 2

Bottom: BC Archives, A-02051

Page 59:   Top: BC Archives, A-03786

Bottom left: Canadian Jackdaw, *Gold in the Cariboo*

Bottom right: BC Archives, A-03771

Page 60:   Bar in Mining Camp, ca. 1865, M605, McCord Museum of Canadian History, Montreal

Page 61:   Top: BC Archives, G-00817

Bottom: with permission from Alden and Cali Hackman, Tim Crosby, photographer

Page 63:   Chinese Gold Washers on the Fraser River, B.C., ca. 1864, M609, McCord Museum of Canadian History, Montreal

Page 64:   BC Archives, F-08550

Page 66:   Left: *Cariboo Sentinel*, 1868

Right: Howay, *British Columbia*, vol. 2

Page 67:   National Archives of Canada, A-0611940

Page 68:   Top: *Cariboo Sentinel*, 1868

Bottom: Howay, *British Columbia*, vol. 2

Page 69:   BC Archives, PDP 003696

Page 70:   Top: *Canadian Illustrated News*, 1872
           Bottom: Howay, *British Columbia*, vol. 2

Page 71:   Top: Howay, *British Columbia*, vol. 2
           Bottom: *Illustrated London News*, 1865

Page 72:   Top: Howay, *British Columbia*, vol. 2
           Bottom left: *Cariboo Sentinel*, 1868
           Bottom right: Howay, *British Columbia*, vol. 2

Page 73:   Top: BC Archives, G-02520
           Bottom: Howay, *British Columbia*, vol. 2

Page 74:   National Archives of Canada, C-001129

Page 75:   Howay, *British Columbia*, vol. 2

Page 76:   Vancouver Museum Archives

Page 77:   National Archives of Canada, C-007846

Page 78:   Top: *Canadian Illustrated News*, 1873
           Bottom: *Harper's Weekly, 1865*

Page 79:   National Archives of Canada, C-088876

Page 80:   Top: Clayton & Co., London, 1865
           Bottom: *Harper's Weekly*, 1865

Page 81:   Top: Howay, *British Columbia*, vol. 2
           Bottom: Howay, *British Columbia*, vol. 2

Page 82: *Canadian Illustrated News*, 1872

Page 83: Howay, *British Columbia*, vol. 2

Page 84: Clayton & Co., London, 1865

Page 85: Top: *Harper's Weekly*, 1865
Bottom: Howay, *British Columbia*, vol. 2

Page 86: *Canadian Illustrated News*, 1876

Page 87: Top: *British Colonist*, 1871
Bottom: Howay, *British Columbia*, vol. 2